CELEBRATE the USA

Hands-On History Activities for Kids

Lynn Kuntz

Illustrated by
Mark A. Hicks

Gibbs Smith, Publisher

TO ENRICH AND INSPIRE HUMANKIND

Salt Lake City | Charleston | Santa Fe | Santa Barbara

First Edition
11 10 09 08 07   5 4 3 2 1

Text © 2006 Lynn Kuntz
Illustrations © 2006 Mark A. Hicks

Published by
Gibbs Smith, Publisher
P.O. Box 667
Layton, Utah 84041

Orders: 1.800.835.4993
www.gibbs-smith.com

Designed by Dawn DeVries Sokol
Printed and bound in China

Library of Congress Cataloging-in-Publication Data
Kuntz, Lynn, 1953-
   Celebrate the USA : hands-on history activities for kids / Lynn Kuntz ; illustrations by Mark A. Hicks. — 1st ed.
      p. cm.
   ISBN-13: 978-1-58685-846-9
   ISBN-10: 1-58685-846-7
   1. United States—History—Juvenile literature. 2. United States—History—Study and teaching—Activity programs. 3.
Creative activities and seat work—Juvenile literature. I. Title.

E178.3.K88 2007
973—dc22

2006021953

DISCLAIMER: Some of the activities suggested in this book require adult assistance and supervision. Children and their parents or guardians should always use common sense and good judgment in playing, cooking, and making crafts. The publisher and author assume no responsibility for any damages or injuries incurred while performing any of the activities in this book; neither are they responsible for the results of these recipes or projects.

To Darryl, my life partner
and best friend—remembering our all-over-the-map American
adventures in Airstream and Poptop!
— Lynn

To Cyanna—
history, art, or science?
—Mark

Contents

Your World, Your Land

Close your eyes. What color is the front door to your home or apartment? How many rooms are inside? Do the walls in your bedroom feel smooth or rough to your fingertips? Are the floors warm or cold under your bare feet? Does your kitchen have a smell all its own? What do you hear through your bedroom windows?

What about the houses on each side of your house, and across the street? Do trees grow strong and tall in the front yards? What does your neighborhood smell like in the summer, fall, winter, and spring? When the sun goes down and daylight fades, what nighttime sounds liven up the dark?

ACTIVITY: Draw a Map of Your World

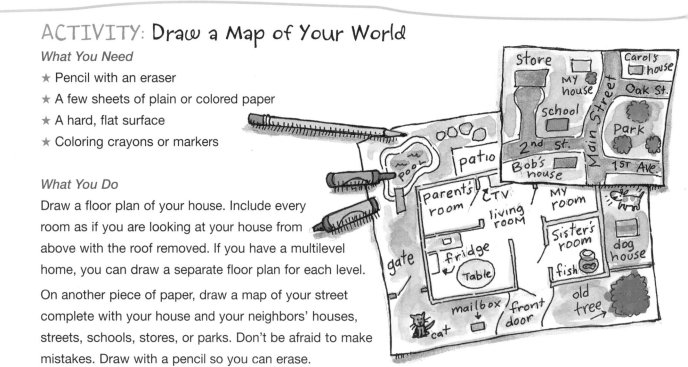

What You Need
★ Pencil with an eraser
★ A few sheets of plain or colored paper
★ A hard, flat surface
★ Coloring crayons or markers

What You Do

Draw a floor plan of your house. Include every room as if you are looking at your house from above with the roof removed. If you have a multilevel home, you can draw a separate floor plan for each level.

On another piece of paper, draw a map of your street complete with your house and your neighbors' houses, streets, schools, stores, or parks. Don't be afraid to make mistakes. Draw with a pencil so you can erase.

Color your pictures.

LIVING IN THE USA

Your home and your neighborhood are at the center of your world—as familiar as family and old friends. You've probably visited other neighborhoods in the city you live in, and maybe traveled around your home state. You might call yourself a New Yorker, a Dallasite, or a Bostonian—an Alaskan, Nebraskan, or Californian. But your home, your neighborhood, your city, and even your state are all part of a larger picture, a larger world that surrounds your smaller world and affects you. It also influences your family's life.

The United States of America (USA) is the larger world that surrounds the smaller world of your state, town, street, and home. When you think of America, you might picture the stars and stripes of our country's flag or hear the words of the Pledge of Allegiance. You might think of noisy parades with men and women in military uniforms. You might be able to almost smell July 4th fireworks. You might think of the Statue of Liberty or hear that "gives-ya-goosebumps" song "America the Beautiful" about amber waves of grain.

All these places are as American as apple pie. Or baseball. Or the American Dream. But what do apple pie, baseball, and the American Dream have in common? And what is an "average American"? What makes something "all-American"? Why do we sing about the "land of the free and the home of the brave"?

Celebrate the USA is full of the whos, whats, wheres, whens, and whys of America. As you read this book, you'll come to know your larger world. You'll learn some surprising stories behind famous American symbols like the Liberty Bell and Uncle Sam. You'll uncover little-known flag and fireworks facts. You'll explore "behind-the-scenes" American life and discover that you live in a one-of-a-kind country that offers opportunity unlike any other on the face of the earth!

The Average American: WHO'S THAT?

America is called the "melting pot" of the world. Although that might not sound like a compliment, it's a wonderful thing to be!

EARLY IMMIGRANTS

Many of us come from families who immigrated to America two hundred or more years ago. But some of us came here just a few years (or even days!) ago.

A melting pot is pretty much what it sounds like—a container in which many ingredients are mixed and melted until they're blended smoothly together. Our country is a melting pot because people from all over the world—regardless of wealth, race, religion, language, and customs—come together and create something altogether new. It's kind of like a soup—the more different ingredients you add, the healthier and more interesting the result!

Most history books tell us that the European immigration to the Americas started in 1492 with Christopher Columbus and a band of weary sailors looking for a new way to get to India (on the continent of Asia) from Europe. After months of sailing across the unexplored Atlantic Ocean, most of them were eager to set foot on solid, dry ground that didn't bob around under their feet. When they finally spied land they hooted and hollered with excitement. They thought they'd reached their goal—India!

It was an easy mistake to make because North America wasn't even on a map! Their next big OOPS was dubbing the inhabitants of the new land "Indians." It made no sense once the Europeans realized they hadn't made it to India after all. But the name stuck.

ACTIVITY: Find the North Star

Sailors in Columbus's day relied on the stars to give them direction. Constellations are groups of stars that seem to move across the night sky depending on the season. You can use a star chart to find constellations that are visible at different times of the year.

What You Need

★ A star chart. If you have access to the Internet, do a Google search. Simply type in "star charts." Or go to your local library and check out some books on constellations and the North Star.

★ A night when the weather will be clear and mild. Get a copy of a star chart for that date and time. (Or use a book that gives information about star positions during certain seasons.)

★ A flashlight to see your star chart at night.

Sailors have used the North Star for thousands of years to guide them. When you know which direction is north, you can determine all the other directions. South is always opposite of north. When you're facing north, west is to your left and east is to your right.

What You Do

When the stars come out, go outside with your star chart and face north. Ask an adult to help if you don't know which direction to look.

Compare the chart and the sky. Study the Big Dipper and the Little Dipper (they are the most famous of all the constellations) on the chart. Can you find them in the sky?

Locate the North Star. You'll see it at the end of the handle of the Little Dipper. You can also find it from the Big Dipper. The outside of the dipper, farthest from the handle, is formed by two stars. Imagine a line going from the bottom star up through the top star, and onward. The imaginary line leads to the North Star.

WHAT'S IN A NAME?

There are at least two opinions of how America got its name. Most history books tell us the name came from Amerigo Vespucci, an Italian explorer and a navigator with Christopher Columbus. It seems Amerigo was the first geographer to realize that the Americas (North and South) were separate continents. In 1507, another mapmaker prepared a world map almost entirely from Vespucci's geographic recordings. On this map, the word "America" is written across both continents.

But some research shows that America may have been named after Richard Amerike, an overseas trader from England. English fishermen may have visited the new land before Columbus crossed the Atlantic. As early as 1481, Amerike shipped a load of salt to Newfoundland, and sailors named the area after their boss.

NATIVE AMERICANS

Some of the earliest Americans (now known as Native Americans or American Indians) beat the rest of us to this land by thousands of years. Most scientists believe they walked from the continent of Asia to get here.

Way up close to the North Pole, only fifty-two miles of salty ocean water separate Asia from North America. This is called the Bering Strait. Those earliest immigrants didn't travel by boat or car or bus or airplane like the immigrants in most of our families.

These first immigrants traveled by foot. They walked from Asia right across the Bering Sea to North America without even getting their tootsies wet. But how?

They came during the Ice Age, when much of the world's water was frozen in polar and mountain ice caps. This meant that the level of the sea was lower, so more land showed. The Bering Sea became so shallow that a vast stretch of dry land appeared and connected, or bridged, the two continents. People migrated slowly eastward, so that when the Ice Age ended and the water rose again, they were living on the North American side of the Bering Sea.

During the next umpteen generations, the descendents of those first immigrants—their grandchildren and great grandchildren—kept right on walking all across America. They became some of the many different tribes of Native Americans that still live in the United States today.

These earliest Americans didn't have an alphabet, so they couldn't leave a written history of their activities in words. Instead they told their life stories by painting and carving bold and graceful pictures in caves and on rocks.

Some of the stories are obvious—a daring and dramatic buffalo hunt, for example, re-created on canyon and cave walls, tells an easily understood tale that could be passed down from one generation to the next. Other drawings show people with unusual headdresses or include intricate designs that leave people today scratching their heads as to what they might mean.

ACTIVITY: Make Cave Drawings

What You Need

★ Large brown paper grocery bag torn into big pieces

★ A black charcoal drawing stick and white chalk. Or different colors of chalk. Or thick crayons, especially brown, white, yellow, and red.

What You Do

To make a background like a cave wall, take a large piece of brown paper bag outside and lay it on a dry sidewalk, a back porch, or a rough piece of wood.

Gently rub your torn piece of paper bag with the charcoal or crayon—use the side, not the tip—to pick up the texture of the sidewalk or wood. Do this coloring lightly, as you will want to draw pictures over this background.

Take your paper inside and place it on the table. Choose white chalk or a different color crayon.

Decide what story you want to tell. It can be something you have experienced—like climbing a tree, catching a butterfly, going fishing, camping outdoors, or seeing a wild animal. It can be something that you think should be important every day to everyone, even something as simple as the sun coming up over the mountains or a clear running stream that provides us with life-giving water.

Now, by using simple symbols, draw your story. Use stick figures, circles, and triangles. Draw the sun and mountains or a stream and trees. You can draw a net and butterfly or a fish and boat. Or draw yourself hiding behind a bush to look at a deer.

THE PROMISED LAND

Soon after Columbus introduced the Old World to the New World, Spanish explorers came to America. They'd heard rumors of fabulously rich cities built entirely of gold. Even though they never found golden cities (that's a rumor for you!) many of them stayed and started families and made America home.

European families began settling in America on a beautiful spring morning in 1607 when three English ships, the *Susan Constant, Godspeed,* and *Discovery,* dropped anchor offshore what is now the state of Virginia. Three passengers took a small boat to shore to check things out.

"Fair meadows, and goodly tall trees, with such fresh waters as almost ravished us to see," was how John Percy enthusiastically described what they'd seen when he returned to the ship. He added that the forests were noble, the birds richly colored, and the ground carpeted with flowers. There were plenty of game birds for good eating, with "stores of turkey nests and many eggs," oysters that were "very large and delicate in taste," and strawberries "four times bigger and better than ours in England."

One hundred and two Pilgrims sailed on the *Mayflower* and 102 arrived in America. Although one Pilgrim adult had died at sea, one Pilgrim child had been born.

It sounded like the "Promised Land" to a lot of folks back home. In 1620, the Pilgrims arrived after two seasick, wave-tossed months at sea on a ship called the *Mayflower*. Many of the Pilgrims had left England to escape mistreatment (prison or even death) because of their religious beliefs.

They had been fortunate on the voyage, but half the Pilgrims died that first difficult winter in the New World. Two Native Americans, Squanto and Massasoit, helped the Pilgrims. Their tribe welcomed the Pilgrims as friends. They showed them where to hunt for birds and game, and how to plant and care for new crops like corn and pumpkins, squash and berries.

Without the help of the Native Americans, the Pilgrims probably would not have survived. After the Pilgrims' first harvest, they gave thanks to God and celebrated with a three-day feast. It was the very first American Thanksgiving.

Thank you! Thank you! Thank you!

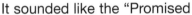

The <u>very</u> <u>first</u> Thanksgiving.

UNCHARTED WILDERNESS

More immigrant families soon followed. But braving the stormy Atlantic Ocean was not a light-hearted adventure. On some immigrant ships, more than half the passengers died at sea. As the Pilgrims had learned, America wasn't exactly paradise—many more immigrants died soon after they arrived.

Northern colonies were bitter cold in winter. The South was hot and suffocating in summer. Most colonists were homesick and missed their families—moms and dads, brothers and sisters, cousins and aunts and uncles—who stayed behind in the Old Country. Most of these new Americans would never again see or hear from their family members in England and Europe.

Building a life in the unknown and unpredictable wilderness that was America was dirty and dangerous work. Vicious wild animals might attack without warning. Never-before-imagined snakes could strike and kill in seconds. Settlers had to hack and claw and scramble their way through dense forests that had never known the blade of an axe. There were no maps for them to follow. They had to figure out which way to go all on their own, with little more than the stars to tell them what direction they were headed.

ACTIVITY: Make a Compass

You've already done an activity to help you find the North Star. Sailors and explorers also use compasses to determine which way is north. Here's how to make your own compass:

What You Need

- ★ Aluminum pie dish
- ★ Liquid dishwashing detergent
- ★ Large sewing needle
- ★ Bar magnet with north end marked (You can get this at any hardware store)

- ★ Small, thick, coin-shaped piece of cork—a bottle cork will work if you cut it so it is wider than it is tall (if it's taller than it is wide, it will tip over on its side)

What You Do

Fill the pie dish two-thirds full of water.

Squirt a few drops of liquid dishwashing detergent into it.

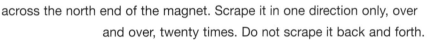

Magnetize the needle by scraping all of it, from tip to tip, across the north end of the magnet. Scrape it in one direction only, over and over, twenty times. Do not scrape it back and forth.

Stick the needle through the cork from one side to the other (not from top to bottom).

Caution: Be careful not to poke your fingers when putting the needle in the cork!

Float the cork in the pie dish. It will immediately turn so the needle is pointing north.

WE ALL HAVE HISTORY

An "average" American's family may have come from Africa, Asia, the British Isles, Europe, India, the Middle East, Polynesia, or South America. The average American might be Christian or Hindu or Buddhist or Muslim or Jewish. He or she might believe in several gods or in no god at all. We Americans have ties to all the countries, languages, and religions of the world.

Regardless of their birthplace, native language, or skin color, our grandparents, aunts, uncles, and other relatives connect us to our heritage, or roots. From these roots we grow into unique individuals, but the roots continue to connect us to the members of our family—past, present, and future. Whether your family came to America during the Ice Age or during the twenty-first century, your family tree is full of people who make you both an average American and a unique American.

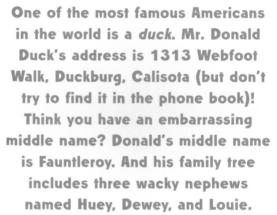

One of the most famous Americans in the world is a *duck*. Mr. Donald Duck's address is 1313 Webfoot Walk, Duckburg, Calisota (but don't try to find it in the phone book)! Think you have an embarrassing middle name? Donald's middle name is Fauntleroy. And his family tree includes three wacky nephews named Huey, Dewey, and Louie.

ACTIVITY: Make a Fabric Family Tree

What You Need

★ White paper and pencil

★ Free pattern (see p. 80)

★ Fabric "blocks" or scraps of fabric in different colors (each about the size of a piece of paper). Choose blue, brown, green, red, and white. (With these colors you can make a family "apple" tree.) Or choose other colors you like. You can also use paper if you don't have fabric, or you can simplify the activity by just drawing the tree with its branches and leaves (use the patterns provided or draw freehand).

★ Straight pins

★ Sharp fabric scissors (Ask an adult for help when cutting fabric.)

★ Tacky glue (a thick white glue that works quickly on fabric) or regular white glue

★ Fine- or medium-point black permanent marker

What You Do First

On your piece of paper, write down the first and last name of your grandmother and your grandfather (choose from your mother's or father's side of the family, but not both sides).

Now, list only the FIRST names of your grandparents' children. This would include your father (or mother) and his (or her) sisters and/or brothers (these are your aunts and uncles).

Next, list the names of each one of your aunts' and uncles' spouses, if they're married. Of course, write down your mom's (or dad's) name too.

Last, list all the names of the children of those couples (these are your cousins). Remember to include your name and your brothers and/or sisters too.

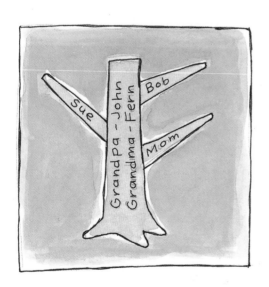

What You Do Next

Choose a large background piece of fabric. From a brown piece of fabric, cut out a tree trunk and as many branches as the number of children your grandparents have. If you'd like, use the pattern on p. 80.

With the black marker, write down the first names of your grandfather and grandmother in the middle of the big tree trunk. Spread tacky glue on the back of the trunk and glue it to the center of the background fabric, close to the bottom edge.

On each branch you cut out, write the first name of each of your grandparents' children. Glue the branches onto the fabric so they look like they are growing from the trunk.

What You Do Last

From a green piece of fabric, cut out a leaf for the spouse (husband or wife) of the person listed on each branch. Use the pattern if you'd like. Write down one name on each leaf. Glue each leaf next to the correct partner's name on each branch.

Now, count up your cousins and siblings and cut out one small apple (or even a cherry if you have a lot of them) for each one. Write one name on each apple.

Using the marker, draw stems along each branch. At the ends of the stems, glue the correct apples (or cherries) to go along with the right parents.

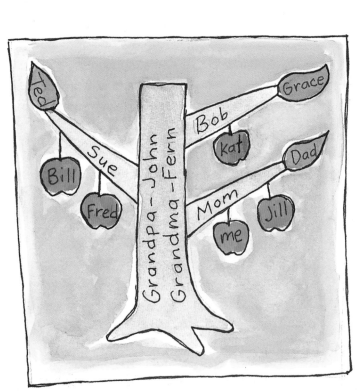

After you've finished with everyone's names, you can add some more green leaves to the top of your tree until you have great big beautiful branches to sit back and admire.

Breaking Away
FROM ENGLAND

One hundred and fifty years after the *Mayflower* Pilgrims held the first Thanksgiving feast, thirteen American colonies sprouted out of the raw, untamed land. They all belonged to Great Britain.

During colonial times, large British ships sailed into the harbors of colonial American cities like Boston and New York every day. They brought everything the colonists needed that wasn't grown or made in America—cloth for sewing clothes, the flavorful tea the colonists loved, sugar for the familiar recipes they'd brought from home, crop seeds, tools, livestock, and books that sometimes seemed more precious than gold because they were so hard to come by.

The thirteen British colonies were Connecticut, Delaware, Georgia, Maryland, Massachusetts, New Hampshire, New Jersey, New York, North Carolina, South Carolina, Pennsylvania, Rhode Island, and Virginia.

Ever since *Mayflower* days, the colonists had followed British customs, celebrated British holidays, and thought of the British king as their own king. British law was the law of the colonies and English—the language of Great Britain—was spoken everywhere in the thirteen colonies.

But it was inconvenient and inefficient to keep doing everything in America the way it was done in England. Plus, these new Americans left Great Britain and the king's rule for very specific reasons. Over the years, the colonists gradually began doing things in a new way—the American way. They began to feel more American than British.

TASTING LIBERTY

Britain's King George and the powerful men in his government lived lives of luxury, with many comforts and fine things. Luxury is expensive and they'd already squeezed every penny they could out of the poor people of Britain. What's a rich king to do? Take money from American colonists, of course!

The king and his men passed a law forcing the colonists to buy everything they needed only from Britain AND to sell everything they produced only to Britain. Americans lost money because British goods cost more and Britain didn't pay a fair price for American goods.

Spot of tea, anyone?

Colonists became poor while King George grew rich! Americans then refused to buy anything more from Britain (this is called a "boycott"). One million colonists, who normally drank tea twice a day, gave it up—a huge sacrifice because they loved their tea like kids love candy! Colonial women started boiling herbs, berry leaves, and birch tree twigs to make the not-so-yummy drink they called "Liberty Tea."

That got King George's attention! But all he did was add more taxes. Then he sent boatloads of British soldiers to American shores. Colonists were furious about the new taxes and called them the Intolerable

Acts! Angry leaders from all thirteen colonies traveled to Philadelphia, Pennsylvania, for a meeting of the Continental Congress held in the Old State House to voice complaints and come up with a plan to get rid of the taxes and the redcoats.

British soldiers were called redcoats, because—you guessed it—they wore red coats!

> Some party, huh?

A few colonists did more than just boycott tea. One day, as British ships sailed into Boston Harbor, a group of colonists disguised themselves as Native Americans, stomped onboard, smashed 342 cargo crates full of delicious tea, and dumped them all overboard, turning Boston Harbor into a huge tea kettle. Though it was no celebration, this act of rebellion became known as the Boston Tea Party.

ACTIVITY: Make Spearmint Liberty Tea

What You Need

- ★ One bunch of fresh spearmint leaves from the grocery store or a health food store (These are also easy to grow in a container on your porch.)
- ★ Large saucepan
- ★ Medium saucepan

- ★ Strainer or colander
- ★ 3 or 4 large tea cups or mugs
- ★ White or brown sugar
- ★ Cream or milk

What You Do First

If you are not old enough to use the stove yourself, ask an adult for help.

Place 3 to 4 cups of water in the large saucepan.

Clean your spearmint leaves by rinsing them in the sink. Add them to the water.

Heat the water and leaves slowly over low heat. Do not boil. The longer you leave it on the heat, the stronger the tea will be.

Put the empty medium saucepan in the sink. Hold the strainer over the pan. Have an adult help you slowly dump the leaves and tea water into the strainer so that it catches the leaves while the pan catches the yummy tea.

What You Do Next

Let the hot tea cool a while.

Carefully pour the warm tea into cups.

Add white or brown sugar to your liking and stir.

Add cream or milk to your liking and stir.

Enjoy your homemade Liberty Tea!

FIGHTING FOR FREEDOM

At first the leaders of the colonies tried to reason with King George. But he was stubborn and paid no attention to their concerns. Many Americans realized that Britain would never be fair with them and they would have to fight for freedom. They called themselves "patriots" and began gathering guns and ammunition.

War began in April of 1775. The redcoats marched inland from Boston Harbor, searching the countryside for two patriot leaders named John Hancock and Samuel Adams. The soldiers also searched for hidden weapons—if they could get all the guns, the patriots wouldn't be able to fight for their freedom.

When patriot spies discovered the redcoats' plans, they decided to send a warning to fellow colonists. In the middle of the night, they sent a man named Paul Revere to gallop on horseback at breakneck speed from Boston to Lexington, Massachusetts, shouting, "The British are coming, the British are coming!"

The British are coming...

When the redcoats got to Lexington, a small band of well-armed patriots was already there. No one knows who fired the first shot, but in the skirmish that followed, King George's soldiers gunned down eighteen Americans. Eight of them died.

Paul Revere had volunteered to be an "alarm rider." As a silversmith, his job was making spoons. He also made false teeth!

BANG!

Did you hear that?

The first shot fired in Lexington became known as "the shot heard 'round the world." Why? Because that single shot triggered the American Revolution and the creation of the United States of America, a country governed by the people, not by a king or queen. The world has never been the same since.

ACTIVITY: Write a Secret Message

American rebels often sent secret messages to each other about their battle plans. If British soldiers captured a messenger, it could mean doom for the American fight for freedom. So messages were written in secret codes. You can learn to write your own secret messages.

What You Need

★ At least two pieces of copy paper
★ Large black marker
★ A friend to help you out

What You Do First

Decide on your secret message. Keep it short and sweet, such as, "Meet 3:00 Treehouse."

With the marker, write the message on a piece of paper. Make the letters large enough to be seen from two or three feet away.

Flip the paper over. Now, trace over the letters you just wrote. They will come out backwards and not make a bit of sense.

Get your next piece of paper. Lay it over the backward writing and trace the secret message again (this way you won't have the real message on the other side).

Tear up the first piece of paper and throw it away.

What You Do Next

Give your secret (backwards) message to your friend. Ask him or her to quickly try to read it. It will look like gibberish to your friend.

Now have your friend hold the message in front of a mirror. Your backwards message can be read easily as a reflection in the mirror!

Make a bunch of backward mirror writings, fold them up, and give them to your friends to announce a secret meeting or party.

THE AMERICAN REVOLUTION

After the battle at Lexington, the redcoats marched to the nearby town of Concord and encountered more Patriots. Men from both sides were killed. The skirmishes at Lexington and Concord were the first two battles of the American Revolution.

America was at war! The Continental Congress had to act fast. First, they created the Continental Army. George Washington of the Virginia Colony showed up at the next congress meeting already wearing an army uniform, showing he was ready, willing, and able to fight. The congress chose him as the commander in chief of the new American army. Volunteers from all the colonies, even eleven- and twelve-year-old boys, lined up to join the ranks.

The Continental Congress tried one last time to make King George listen to reason. They sent a petition saying they would stay loyal to him if he would just compromise with them. They called it the Olive Branch Petition, because it encouraged King George to choose the olive branch that symbolized peace instead of the sword of war. But King George refused to read the letter.

Great Britain was the most powerful nation in the world, with the most powerful army. The new Continental Army, on the other hand, was mostly a ragtag group of untrained farmers and their sons. They didn't even have uniforms to designate the group or regiment to which they belonged. Washington came up with a temporary solution—sewing colored ribbons on the tricorn (three-cornered) hats all the soldiers wore, using a different color for each group.

WE DECLARE INDEPENDENCE!

During the next year, the Continental Congress became convinced that America's relationship with Great Britain could never be repaired. On June 11, 1776, they agreed to officially declare in writing that the thirteen colonies were taking charge of their own destiny. They called this document the Declaration of Independence.

One of the most important representatives at the Congress was John Adams, who courageously stated, "I am well aware of the toil and blood and treasure it will cost us to maintain this declaration, and support and defend these states. Yet through all the gloom I see the rays of ravishing light and glory. I can see that the end is worth all the means. This is our day of deliverance."

Thomas Jefferson was one of the youngest representatives. He was quiet and didn't say much, but he was a gifted writer. The other men asked him to write the Declaration of Independence, but he was afraid to accept such a huge responsibility. He thought Benjamin Franklin should write it.

A small, crumpled page from one of Jefferson's earliest thrown-away versions was rescued and still exists. It is protected under glass in a museum.

But Jefferson was a true patriot, and when both Franklin and Adams agreed that he was their man, Jefferson accepted the job. The race against time was on! Jefferson attended meetings of the Continental Congress during the day, then wrote like crazy at night. He would often get frustrated when he couldn't think of the perfect words and would rip up pages that had taken him hours to write.

On July 2, 1776, Congress voted to approve the declaration as Jefferson had written it. (Franklin and Adams helped change it a bit until the wording seemed perfect.) Two days later, on July 4, 1776, the final version was voted into law and the United States of America was born.

"I did not consider it part of my charge to invent new ideas, but to place before mankind the common sense of the subject."
—Thomas Jefferson, speaking about the Declaration of Independence

The Declaration of Independence explained the reasons for the colonists' rejection of British rule. It listed the principles that would guide the new nation and make it different from every other country in the world. One of the most important ideas was that all people deserve certain basic privileges, or rights, no matter where they are born, how rich or poor their families are, or what religion they practice. The document also said that governments should work for the good of ALL people, not just the most wealthy and powerful.

The document starts like this: "We hold these truths to be self-evident, that all men are created equal, that they are endowed, by their Creator, with certain unalienable Rights, that among these are Life, Liberty, and the Pursuit of Happiness."

New and revolutionary, these ideas were completely opposed to the way governments all over the world were run. Everywhere else, small groups of wealthy and powerful men controlled everyone else and made all the laws. In contrast, Americans said they should have a government "by the people and for the people."

ACTIVITY: Declare Your List of Rights

What You Need

★ A few pieces of paper

★ A pen or pencil

What You Do

Make a list of rights you think all people, including kids, should have.

Your list might include simple everyday things like the right to:

    ★ climb a tree.

    ★ play with friends.

    ★ go freely and safely outside.

Or you might include more personal rights like the right to:

    ★ have clean clothing and a place to live.

    ★ live without fear, discrimination, or violence.

    ★ go to school and get an education.

    ★ choose the kind of job you want to have.

    ★ live where you want.

    ★ vote for people to represent you in government.

When you're finished, hang your list up on your bedroom wall or door.

WORLD'S BEST INVENTOR

The United States has been a nation of inventors from the very beginning, when we invented a new nation based on ideals and opportunities never before offered in any country in the world.

Benjamin Franklin, one of early America's most important leaders, was also one of America's first and most famous inventors. A brilliant and energetic man, he spent much of his time thinking up things that would make life better and easier for people. He experimented with lightning and invented a lightning rod to protect people from lightning strikes. He experimented with fire and invented the Franklin wood stove—one of the most efficient home-heating systems in America for more than two hundred years.

Another of his experiments involved music. Franklin placed several fancy crystal wine glasses on a table, all in a row. He poured different amounts of water in the glasses. Then he tapped the rims of the wine glasses with a spoon. Identical glasses with different amounts of water produced different musical notes distinct from all the others. Two identical glasses with exactly the same amount of water produced the same note.

Using what he learned in the wine glass experiment, Franklin created a new musical instrument that he called a glass " 'armonica." First he built a wooden box in the shape of a small upright piano. Inside the box, he mounted a rod. A series of glass bowls hung from the rod. The rod was connected to a pedal outside the box. When the pedal was pumped by a person's foot, the rod turned. As the rod turned, the rims of the glass bowls were dipped in a tray of water. The musician playing the instrument then tapped the rims of the bowls to produce musical notes.

This instrument became very popular in America and even in Europe. In fact, two of the most famous composers in Europe— Beethoven and Mozart—composed music for Franklin's glass 'armonica.

ACTIVITY: Make Franklin's Glass "'Armonica"

What You Need

★ Eight identical crystal drinking glasses. Tall, thin ones are best. Be sure to ask an adult's permission!

★ Pitcher
★ Stainless-steel spoon
★ Pencil

What You Do

Line up the glasses in a straight row, an inch or so apart, on a sturdy table or kitchen counter—somewhere they won't get knocked over.

Fill a pitcher with water and pour a small amount of it into the first glass. Add slightly more water to the second glass. Add even more to the third. Add yet more to the fourth. Continue filling the glasses in this way until there is water in all eight glasses.

Wet your pointer finger. Gently run your finger around the rim of each glass to produce a distinct tone. Be patient—it may take some practice before you get the hang of it! You will hear a different note with each glass.

You can also try tapping each glass gently with a spoon to produce a tone.

Can you guess why we suggested eight glasses?

Because with eight glasses you can play "do, re, mi, fa, so, la, ti, do"— the standard eight notes of a musical scale!

If you have a pitch pipe or piano, you can experiment with the amount of water in the first glass until it produces a perfect C note. Once you have a perfect C, you can determine the amount of water the second glass needs to produce a D note, and so on until you can play a full musical scale. Adding or taking away water from a glass will change the tone.

pitch pipe

THE SOUND OF LIBERTY

On July 8, 1776, the bell we now call the Liberty Bell rang long and loud in Philadelphia to beckon all the townspeople to the Old State House. When a large crowd had gathered, the Declaration of Independence was read publicly for the first time. The crowd went wild, shouting and whistling and dancing their approval.

Soon after, the declaration was read in Boston. An enthusiastic crowd mobbed the state house there. They pulled down King George's shield that hung above the big main doors. Instead of crying out, "God Save the King!" as was the custom at public meetings, Bostonians shouted, "God Save the American States!"

On the battlefields, George Washington read the declaration to the troops. They cheered long and loud and threw their tricorn hats high. Then they got busy melting down statues of King George into lead for bullets to be used in the fight against Britain! Signing the declaration was a gutsy move. Each person who signed was targeted as an enemy of King George and the British government. If he was captured by British troops, or if the Americans lost the war, every signer would be hung. Ben Franklin wasn't joking when he observed, "Surely, we must all hang together—or we shall all hang separately!"

Although representatives from every colony eventually signed the Declaration of Independence, only John Hancock and Charles Thomson actually signed on July 4th. John Hancock went first, taking up enough space for twenty signatures. He dipped his feather pen in ink and scrawled his name in giant letters, underlined with a big, fancy flourish. "There!" he said. "King George the Third can read THAT without his spectacles!"

John Hancock

Have you ever been asked for your "John Hancock"? It means you need to sign your name. Do it with gusto, just like that famous founder!

A GREAT SACRIFICE

It was easier to talk about independence than to actually make it happen. The next winter was bitter. Conditions were terrible for the American soldiers. The odds against them were almost overwhelming. George Washington admitted that if he had known how bad it would be, he would have refused to take command.

Many fought barefoot on the frozen ground, blood from their ice-torn feet smearing bright red on the white snow. Those who had shoes sometimes chewed the leather because they were so hungry. Men who fell rarely got up again. Everywhere, American soldiers were dying of disease, cold, and starvation.

Patriot troops were commanded, "Don't fire until you see the whites of their eyes!" It was good advice, because you had to be that close to hit your target with the guns, called muskets, that they used back then.

Americans sacrificed and suffered during the war. In most families at least one husband or brother fought. The families waited fearfully for news of the battles, always worried that their father or son or brother or best friend had died. Farm women and girls had to take over all the jobs their men and boys usually handled. The British often burned entire towns. They took horses, wagons, food, silver, and valuables, and anything else that caught their fancy. They often flattened all the crops on farms and killed all the farm animals they couldn't take with them. They left many families with nothing, doomed to poverty and starvation.

Even though Washington sometimes felt overwhelmed by his responsibility as commander in chief of the Continental Army, his belief that Americans were fighting for what was right was unshakable. The war went on for six long years. To keep his men (and himself) from giving up, Washington often assured them that freedom was worth fighting, and even dying, for.

And in the end, that's why the Americans won. They had one huge advantage over the British: they were fighting for their homes, their families, their neighbors, their communities, and their rights to life, liberty, and the pursuit of happiness.

COLONIAL UNIFORMS

As the war continued, Washington designed a uniform to replace the rags worn by most American soldiers. But a big problem remained—there was no cloth, since it had always been brought by the British ships. Even if they'd had cloth, there were no factories to make uniforms. Thus, patriot women throughout the colonies added the making of uniforms to their long list of chores.

Everything was done by hand, one step at a time. For linen cloth, the colonists grew flax. It took months to plant, water, weed, and harvest. Then they soaked and pounded the flax to produce linen fibers. Then they spun the fibers into thread on a spinning wheel. Getting wool was just as difficult. They sheared the sheep and cleaned the fleece. Then they carded it and spun it into wool thread or yarn.

Once they had enough linen or wool thread, they wove it into cloth. They collected berries and leaves to make dye for the proper uniform colors. They cut the colored cloth into patterns of the right shapes and sizes, and stitched the seams by hand. Even little girls, only four and five years old, worked to make uniforms.

ACTIVITY: Dye Colorful Colonial Clothes

CAUTION: This can be a messy activity. BE SURE to ask an adult to help you. Throughout this activity, wear an old painting shirt and be careful not to splash!

What You Need
★ Patience first—this activity takes two days!
★ Large stainless-steel cooking pot with lid

★ Strainer

★ Large glass bowl

★ Cutting board

★ Chopping and mashing utensils

★ Clothing to dye. Natural fibers work best. Choose undyed cotton or wool like the colonists used. A white cotton T-shirt or white socks work well.

★ Plants for different colored dyes:

    Beets—deep pinkish red

    Grass or spinach—green

    Carrots—yellow

    Coffee or chocolate—brown

    Purple grape juice—violet to purple

    Tomato juice—orange

The dyes you'll be working with can permanently stain anything in your work area, including kitchen dishcloths, countertops, sinks, and your clothes, so work slowly and with care!

What You Do First

Wash your clothing item (even if it's new) with detergent. This will remove dirt and oil that might keep the dye from setting in evenly. Don't use fabric softener because it interferes with dye. Let the clothing air-dry (don't use a clothes dryer) while you do the next step.

Chop or smash the tough and fibrous plant or plants you want to use. Choose only one or two at first. Process each one individually so you don't mix colors.

Put each pile of colorful "mush" into a glass bowl and add enough water to cover. Soak overnight.

After overnight soaking, transfer plant chunks and liquid to a stainless steel cooking pot.

Heat the mixture to boiling, and then put a lid on the pot and simmer over the lowest heat for about an hour. As the liquid heats, some will evaporate and you may need to add more water. The less water used, the deeper the color. The more water used, the lighter the color.

Shortcut: You can skip steps 2 and 3 if you're using juices like grape or tomato. But keep in mind that the colonists didn't have such shortcuts—they had to do everything "from scratch"!

What You Do Next

After an hour of simmering, turn off the heat and take the lid off

the pot. Let the dye cool so you won't get burned.

An adult should pour the dye through the strainer into a large stainless-steel pot or stainless-steel sink. If the pot you cooked the dye in is large enough, you can leave the dye in it. But remove all the plant parts.

Stir the dye well, then submerge your clothing item into the dye. Stir to make sure the dye covers the clothing evenly.

Stir for five minutes; then drain.

Squeeze out additional liquid and hang your dyed clothing outside to dry.

Wash your hands with soap right away to remove any dye.

All-American
SYMBOLS

If you attend school or belong to a club, you already know about symbols. A symbol is something that stands for, or represents, something else. A heart shape is a symbol of love. A four-leaf clover is a symbol of good luck. An evergreen wreath with red bows is a symbol of Christmas.

If your school's sports team is called the Mustangs, for example, it might be symbolized by a galloping wild horse design on the school uniforms or the scoreboard in the gymnasium.

Being part of a school or club can give a group of people a shared sense of purpose and a feeling of belonging. Schools and clubs are communities. A community is simply a group of people who share something in common—they might share space (a school, neighborhood, state, or country) or common interests (love horses, hate to dance, crazy about computers or TV). They might share common values or a common history.

A country is a large community of people who usually share space AND common interests AND common values AND common history. Countries, like other communities, choose symbols to represent them.

STARS AND STRIPES FOREVER

A country's flag often becomes its most important and well-known symbol. A flag says something important about a country and its people.

The Continental Congress first met in 1774. Members from all thirteen colonies met in Philadelphia, Pennsylvania, to share their complaints about King George and his taxes. The

Continental Congress approved the design for the very first American flag in 1775, when the colonies still belonged to Great Britain. This flag was called the Grand Union. It featured a flag within a flag because it included a small version of the Union Jack, Britain's flag. King George approved of the Grand Union because the miniature Union Jack in the upper left corner showed the whole world that the American colonies belonged to Britain. But we know that didn't last long.

Grand Union

Just a year later, not many Americans wanted to belong to Britain anymore. American colonists finally had all they could take of bossy King George, so they fought for—and won—the right to be a free and independent nation. These newly independent Americans wanted a brand-new flag for their brand-new nation.

The Continental Congress of 1777 decided the first flag of the United States should feature thirteen stripes and thirteen stars. The stripes represented the thirteen colonies. The stars represented the thirteen states the colonies became. They were arranged in a circle to show they were all equal, with none deserving a more important place than the others.

Congress chose colors to symbolize values. Red stands for strength, bravery, and victory; white for purity, honesty, and fairness; and blue for vigilance, loyalty, and perseverance.

"Let the thirteen stars in a circle stand as a new constellation in the heavens."
—George Washington

BETSY MADE OUR FLAG

Many historians believe an American seamstress named Betsy Ross created the first flag of the United States. Here's how they think it happened:

Betsy's husband had died and she was a single parent, working hard to support her family. She sewed all sorts of things, including window curtains and furniture upholstery. George Washington knew of Betsy's talent with a needle and thread because she had sewn clothing for him. He showed her a rough sketch of a design for the new flag. The sketch originally had stars with six points because he thought five-pointed stars would be too difficult to sew, especially with thirteen of them. But Betsy wowed him when, with just a few folds and snips, she produced a beautiful five-pointed star.

Vigilance **means standing guard over our ideals and freedoms.** *Perseverance* **means hanging in there, even when it's hard.**

Betsy worked far into the night, squinting as she snipped and stitched stars and stripes in the dim candlelight. It was important to get the flag flying high to unite and inspire Americans. With their very own flag for encouragement, they'd be able to make the sacrifices necessary for their newborn nation to survive and prosper.

We Americans have an affectionate nickname for our flag—Old Glory. In 1831, when America was still "the new kid on the block," a ship's captain sailed away from Massachusetts on a world voyage. His friends gave him an American flag as a going-away gift. At that time, the flag had 24 stars. As the captain's ship skimmed across the open sea, the beautiful red, white, and blue flag unfurled and waved majestically in the breeze. "Old Glory!" the captain exclaimed in appreciation. The name stuck.

ACTIVITY: Make a Betsy Ross Five-Pointed Star

Thanks to the Betsy Ross House for providing these instructions.

What You Need

★ A thin piece of paper 8½" x 10" (not 8½" x 11")
★ Scissors

What You Do

1. Fold an 8½" x 10" piece of paper in half.

Step 1

2. Fold and unfold in half both ways to form creased center lines.

Step 2

3. Bring corner (1) right to meet the center line. Be sure to fold from the vertical crease line.

4. Bring corner (1) left till edges coincide, then make the fold.

5. Bring corner (2) left and fold.

6. Bring corner (2) right until edges coincide. Then fold.

7. Cut on the angle as shown in the picture. Then unfold the small piece.

Step 2

Step 3

8. Marvel at your perfect (we hope!) 5-pointed star! If your star is not perfect, take a fresh piece of paper (8½" x 10" — not 8½" x 11") and return to Step 1.

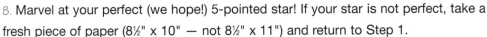

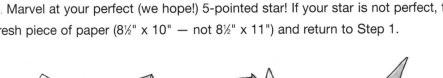

Step 4

Step 5

Step 6

Step 7

Finished!

ACTIVITY: Bake a Very Berry Flag Cake

You can design a red, white, and blue flag on top of a cake by using white whipped topping, straw-berries, and blueberries.

What You Need

★ 1 box white cake mix (or your favorite flavor)

★ Rectangular cake pan

★ 3 cups fresh strawberries

★ 1 cup fresh blueberries

★ 2 cups frozen whipped topping, thawed

What You Do First

With an adult assistant and following the directions on the cake mix box, mix and bake your favorite cake in a rectangular pan. Let the cake cool completely in the pan.

Place the cake, still in the pan, into the refrigerator for about 30 minutes to make sure it gets cold and will not melt the whipped topping.

While the cake is cooling, rinse and prepare the strawberries. Cut off the stem tops, and then slice the strawberries lengthwise. Ask an adult for help. Set them aside in a bowl.

Rinse the fresh blueberries. Set aside in a bowl.

What You Do Next

Take the cake out of the fridge, but leave it in the pan.

Spread whipped topping over the top of the cake.

Arrange blueberries in the upper left corner of the cake to resemble the blue and white field of stars on our nation's flag. Just put the blueberries in lines to make a square. For the stars, leave areas open for the whipped cream to show through.

Now arrange the strawberries in long lines across the white topping, leaving white space (for a white stripe) between each red stripe.

Show off your finished cake. Then cut it up and share it!

Our flag has been flown at some interesting places, including the North Pole, Mount Everest, and even the Moon.

AN EAGLE SOARS

Around the same time our country's founders decided on a design for our flag, they chose the bald eagle as a national symbol. Most of our founders were born and raised in Great Britain, where wild birds and animals "belonged to" the ruling class—the rich and important people. It was exciting to early Americans to think that the incredible variety of wild creatures in the newborn nation belonged equally to all Americans.

Bald eagles are extra-special to Americans because they live only in our part of the world. Adult bald eagles have dark brown bodies with pure white heads and tails. The dramatic contrast makes them easy to spot and identify. They have amazingly long wing spans. They're strong and fierce fighters. Soaring high, fast, and free, they're among the most independent of all birds. Our founders approved of these qualities and believed they represented the American spirit.

Our flag of stars and stripes has become the most important symbol of the United States of America. It is known all around the world.

As America grew, many more states joined the Union. In 1818, Congress decreed that the flag would continue to have thirteen stripes to represent the original colonies but that a star would be added to the flag every time a new state was added to the country.

So how many stars brighten our flag today? Fifty. How many states make up the United States of America? You don't even have to do the math—it's the same number! The fiftieth star was added in July 1960, for Hawaii, which is our fiftieth state.

Another bird Americans know and love (to eat) almost became our national bird! When our founders thought about choosing a national bird, Ben Franklin tried to persuade them to pick the wild turkey. He called the turkey "respectable" and a "bird of courage." He criticized the more noble-looking bald eagle for being a scavenger and stealing food from other birds. In Franklin's exact words, the bald eagle was "too lazy to fish for himself!" But, let's admit it, the bald eagle is much better looking than a turkey!

Why are bald eagles called "bald" when their heads are covered with white feathers?

The Old English word *balde* means white. This was a familiar word to the colonists.

THE GREAT SEAL OF THE UNITED STATES

In 1782, Congress chose the bald eagle as the main feature in the design for the first Great Seal of the United States. A seal is a stamp with a cut or raised design that can be pressed into wax or paper. The Great Seal is like a signature of the USA. It makes a special mark on official documents to show they're actually from the government of the United States of America.

Long before Europeans came to America, Native Americans admired the power and majesty of bald eagles. They often carved them in places of honor at the tops of totem poles. Many tribal people prized eagle feathers, believing prayers would soar straight to heaven with their help. Bald eagle feathers are still used in traditional tribal ceremonies, including the beautiful Eagle Dance. It's also a favorite at powwows.

The seal shows a bald eagle with its head turned to the side and its wings spread wide. It holds an olive branch with thirteen leaves and thirteen olives, symbolizing peace, in the talons of one foot. It holds thirteen arrows in the sharp talons of its other foot, symbolizing America's strength and ability to protect itself. These two symbols together say that we are a peace-loving nation but we won't let anyone push us around!

The eagle holds a banner in its beak with the words *E Pluribus Unum* written across it. The words are Latin, meaning "Out of many, one." This refers to the many (thirteen) colonies becoming one nation.

A ring of clouds floats above the eagle's head. In the center are thirteen stars on a blue background. Beams of light shine out from the stars. Can you guess what these might symbolize? A shield covers most of the eagle's body between its head and tail. A horizontal bar of blue crosses the top third. It symbolizes the colonies joined together. Thirteen vertical red and white stripes fill the bottom two thirds of the shield.

Thirteen stars, thirteen stripes, thirteen olive leaves, arrows, and olives—by now you know that symbols in groups of thirteen are

repeated over and over and stand for the thirteen colonies, which became the first thirteen states of the United States of America.

The back of the Great Seal features a pyramid built with thirteen rows of stones. An eye, the all-seeing eye of God, watches over the pyramid. The year of our country's birth, 1776, is written in Roman numerals (MDCCLXXVI) at the bottom of the pyramid.

Two mottos, written in Latin, are etched on the seal: *Annuit Coeptis* translates to, "He has smiled on our undertakings," meaning that God has favored and blessed the United States, and *Novus Ordo Seclorum* translates to, "A new order of the ages." In other words, the creation of the United States marks the beginning of a new way of life. For the first time, government will be chosen BY the people and will work for the benefit of ALL the people.

Only the front of the Great Seal is used as an official "signature." Want to see what it looks like? Look on the back of a $1 bill. You'll see the designs from both the front and back of the Great Seal.

ACTIVITY: Create a Club Seal

What You Need
★ Your imagination
★ Pencil
★ Paper
★ Crayons or markers
★ (Optional: Scissors, glue, and different colors of fabric)

What You Do

Think of something you're interested in and imagine you're starting a club for people who share your interest. It might be the Animal Lover's Club, the Chocolate Chip Cookie Fan Club, the Electric Train Collectors' Club, or the Stinky Sweaty Sock-Sniffing Club. What is your fantasy club?

Make up a motto, or saying, for your club. For example, if you have a Neighborhood Cleanup Club, your motto might be, "A waste-basket a day keeps the litter away." If you like the Puppy Dog Fan Club, your motto might be "Pamper Your Pup." The Couch Potatoes' Club motto could be "My Turf to Channel Surf."

Invent a symbol for your club. The symbol for the Neighborhood Cleanup Club might be a wadded up gum wrapper with a big red X over it. The Puppy Dog Fan Club might be symbolized by a set of chubby puppy paw prints in a heart shape. You can take it from here!

Now make a sign with all three items: your club name, your motto, and your symbol (sometimes called a logo). You can color it or even use the skills you learned earlier in the Family Tree activity to make a club flag, complete with your seal.

RING IN THE NEW WORLD

The Liberty Bell was a fairly ordinary bell before the American Revolution. It came to fame just because it was in the right place at the right time—hanging in the tower of the Pennsylvania State House above the room where the Continental Congress voted the United States of America into being.

The Liberty Bell was inscribed with the words "Proclaim liberty throughout all the land unto all the inhabitants thereof." These words came from the book of Leviticus in the Bible—and they turned out to be prophetic (meaning that they foretold something that would happen in the future)! It was the Liberty Bell's repeated ringing that called the citizens of Philadelphia to the

State House to hear the first public reading of the Declaration of Independence. Because the bell played a unique role in history, it became a lasting symbol of freedom.

So why was the Liberty Bell in the State House to begin with? In 1751, twenty-five years before the American Revolution, the leaders of the Pennsylvania Colony ordered a bell to be made for the Pennsylvania State House, which was their meeting place. They wanted the bell to honor the fifty-year anniversary of Pennsylvania Colony's Constitution, a document stating that people everywhere should be free.

The State House bell was made in London. Then it was sent to Pennsylvania Colony. It appeared to be in perfect shape and the colonists liked what they saw. But when it was rung for the very first time, C-R-A-C-K!

Assemblyman Isaac Norris described what happened this way: "I had the mortification to hear that it was cracked by a stroke of the clapper without any other violence as it was hung up to try the sound."

OOPS.

Two metal workers named Mr. Stow and Mr. Pass melted the bell and remolded it. To make the new bell stronger, they mixed some extra copper into the melted metal.

Unfortunately, the new bell's peal, or sound, was horrible! Folks made so many jokes about its silly sound that Stow and Pass smashed it up, melted it over a fire, and molded it again. People didn't like the peal of the third version, either. Pennsylvanians are hard to please.

CRACK!

Mr. Norris requested and received a brand-new bell from London, but its peal was even worse. Finally, the colonists gave up their quest for a regal-sounding bell and just hung the Stow-and-Pass redo.

From then on, they only rang the Liberty Bell to call the Assembly to meeting and to notify citizens of special events or announcements. It rang, for instance, when King George became king of England in 1761. It rang when Benjamin Franklin traveled to England to tell King George of the colonists' complaints. It rang to announce the meeting of the First Continental Congress in 1774, after the Battles of Lexington and Concord. Finally—and most famously—it rang after the Continental Congress declared American independence.

During the Revolutionary War, the bell was taken down and hidden. After the war it was re-hung in Philadelphia and rung on important occasions, including every Fourth of July. Going . . . going . . . gong—the Liberty Bell cracked again in 1835. It rang for the last time on George Washington's birthday in 1846.

Today this famous American symbol hangs in the Liberty Bell Pavilion at Independence National Historical Park in Philadelphia, Pennsylvania. Although it hasn't been rung in more than 150 years, it's been "struck" on many special occasions. And every year on the Fourth of July, in a special ceremony, children who are descendants of the men who signed the Declaration of Independence tap the bell thirteen times (and you know why!).

The Liberty Bell cost about $300— a LOT of money in those days.

ACTIVITY: Bake Liberty Bell Cookies

What You Need

★ Wax paper

★ ¼ cup flour

★ 1 roll of slice-and-bake sugar cookie dough

★ Rolling pin

★ Bell-shaped cookie cutter

★ Cooking spray

★ Cookie sheet

★ Hot pads

★ Spatula

★ Serving platter or large plate

★ Butter knife

★ Container of red, white, or blue store-bought frosting

★ Tube of icing (for writing), in one of the colors you didn't choose for the main frosting

What You Do First

Put some wax paper on a clean kitchen counter or table.

Sprinkle flour lightly across the wax paper and roll out the cookie dough with a rolling pin to about ¼ inch thickness.

Use the cookie cutter to cut out bell shapes.

Lightly spray cooking spray on the cookie sheet.

Place the bell cookies on the cookie sheet.

What You Do Next

Bake according to the cookie-dough package instructions. Keep an eye on them so they don't burn.

With an adult assistant, use hot pads to remove the cookie sheet from the oven. Let cookies cool a bit, but not fully. Lift them off with a spatula and place them on a serving platter.

Using a butter knife, cover the cookies with a layer of frosting.

Using your tube of icing, draw a crooked line starting from the bottom to about halfway up each Liberty Bell cookie to resemble the famous crack.

An Uncle Named Sam

Sometimes we choose our symbols—and sometimes they "choose" us. "Uncle Sam" is probably the most famous American in the world. Dressed in energetic red, white, and blue, with long, skinny legs, a small, white beard and jaunty top hat with stars on it, he's quite a character. But where did this odd-looking guy come from?

Though the Uncle Sam we know and love is not a real person, his character is based on a real person—a man named Sam Wilson who supplied American soldiers with meat during the War of 1812, when the U.S. fought the British for the second time. Wilson, whose nickname was Uncle Sam, delivered crates of meat stamped with the initials U and S, to show they were for United States troops. The letters also happen to be the initials for Uncle Sam.

Pretty soon soldiers called the U.S. stamp Uncle Sam's stamp. Before long, they called the United States government "Uncle Sam." A cartoon version of Uncle Sam began appearing in newspapers to represent things the government was doing.

More than a century and a half later, nobody remembers much about the real Samuel Wilson. But he lives on, in a way, as the person who inspired America's national cartoon hero, Uncle Sam.

LARGER THAN LIFE

Lady Liberty, as the Statue of Liberty is often called, makes the famous basketball player Shaquille O'Neal look like a shrimp. (She is 52 times taller than Shaq!) If you stood next to her nose, it would probably be taller than you! (It measures 4 feet, 6 inches—one little sneeze and you could be in big trouble!)

The Statue of Liberty was a birthday present, the biggest ever, given to the United States by the country of France. It was dedicated in 1886. A famous French sculptor named Bartholdi designed her to represent the ideals set forth in the Declaration of Independence—and also to commemorate the friendship between Americans and the French that began when France helped the colonists defeat the British during the American Revolution.

From the soles of her sandals to the top of her head, Lady Liberty stands 151 feet 1 inch tall. Her hand measures 16 feet, 5 inches; her index finger 8 feet; the fingernail, 13 inches by 10. Her sandals are 25 feet long—which would be like a size 879 shoe!

Lady Liberty's official name is Liberty Enlightening the World. Straight and strong, she stands atop tiny Liberty Island, at the entrance to busy New York Harbor. Her watchful face has been the first glimpse of America for millions of immigrants as they head by boat to nearby Ellis Island, where they first set foot on U.S. soil.

Dressed in flowing robes, Lady Liberty resembles a goddess from ancient Rome. Broken chains, symbolizing the cruel conditions of life in many of the countries immigrants came from, are crushed beneath her feet. Spikes radiate from her crown like glowing rays of sunlight.

She grasps a flaming torch in her 42-foot-long, outstretched arm, to welcome and symbolically guide the immigrants' passage from the dim prospects of life in the "old country" to America, a land of unlimited opportunity. In her other arm, she holds a garage-sized tablet, etched with the date July 4, 1776.

"THE NEW COLOSSUS"

On a plaque at the base of the statue is a poem written by Emma Lazarus in 1883 titled "The New Colossus." It's fairly long, but you'll get a good idea of what Lady Liberty stands for—and what a powerful symbol she has become—when you read even a few lines from it:

"Here at our sea-washed, sunset gates shall stand
A mighty woman with a torch, whose flame
Is the imprisoned lightning, and her name
Mother of Exiles. From her beacon-hand
Glows world-wide welcome . . . "

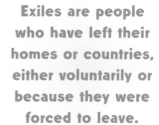

Exiles are people who have left their homes or countries, either voluntarily or because they were forced to leave.

A little later in the poem, Lady Liberty says to the world,
"Give me your tired, your poor,
Your huddled masses yearning to breathe free,
The wretched refuse of your teeming shore."

Those are the most famous lines of the poem. Almost as famous are the final lines in which Lady Liberty says, "Send these, the homeless, tempest-tost, to me, I lift my lamp beside the golden door!"

NOT JUST WHISTLIN' DIXIE

In the 1850s, just before the Civil War, the American government made paper money in several different places, including New Orleans, Louisiana. In those days, French was spoken there as often as English, since France had owned much of Louisiana before it became part of the United States.

The words printed on the money were a mixture of English and French. The French word for ten, "dix" was printed on the back of the $10 bill. Louisiana became known as the land of the Dixes, or Dixies. The Southern states became known as Dixieland.

The American dollar has become a symbol of our country. It is recognized and respected around the world. In fact, it's often used to set a standard—people of other countries compare the value of their own money to the American dollar to determine if their country's economy is healthy.

Look for our country's motto, In God We Trust, printed on American money.

FUN MONEY FACTS

There are two one-dollar coins. One pictures Susan B. Anthony, a woman who fought for women's rights. The other is the color of gold and shows the American Indian guide, Sacagawea, holding a baby or "papoose."

Can you name two other women whose pictures have appeared on U.S. currency?

Martha Washington and Pocahontas

Rub some dollar bills of any amount between your fingers. If you think dollars are made out of paper, think again! What are your three best guesses?

They're made out of cotton.

ACTIVITY: Match Money to Mugs

What You Need

★ Matching game on page 53

★ Pencil or pen

★ As many different bills and coins as you can find (Be sure to ask before borrowing someone else's money!)

What You Do

Draw a line from each famous American's face to the bill or coin it matches. Some faces match both a bill and a coin.

Answers:

1. Benjamin Franklin: $100 bill
2. President George Washington: $1 bill and quarter (25¢)
3. President John F. Kennedy: silver half dollar (50¢)
4. President Ulysses S. Grant: $50 bill
5. President Abraham Lincoln: $5 bill and penny (1¢)
6. President Thomas Jefferson: nickel (5¢)
7. Alexander Hamilton: $10 bill
8. President Andrew Jackson: $20 bill
9. President Franklin Roosevelt: dime (10¢)

1. Benjamin Franklin

2. George Washington

3. John F. Kennedy

4. Ulysses S. Grant

5. Abraham Lincoln

6. Thomas Jefferson

7. Alexander Hamilton

8. Andrew Jackson

9. Franklin Roosevelt

Songs, Sayings
AND SPEECHES

Like our national symbols, all-American songs, sayings, and speeches inspire and encourage us. They guide the way we live our lives. They influence our decisions. They unite us. They strengthen and steady us during difficult times.

During the War of 1812, British ships attacked Washington, D.C. From as far away as Baltimore, Maryland, Americans could see flames engulfing our nation's capital. After pounding D.C., the British beelined to Maryland to attack American troops at Fort McHenry. They bombarded them with more than 2,100 bombs and rockets for twenty-five horrific hours.

Francis Scott Key, an American lawyer, saw the battle from a ship. The air was thick with smoke from the booming cannons. All night long muskets roared and rockets shrieked and flashed in a deadly fireworks display. Each time the sky lit up, Key tried to catch a glimpse of the huge American flag that always flew above the walls of Fort McHenry. If the flag was still flying, it meant the Americans were still fighting. If it went down, it meant the Americans had surrendered. Finally dawn came. Key strained to see through the smoky haze of battle. He felt as if his heart would burst with joy when he spotted Old Glory—still waving proudly. He wrote his thoughts on the only paper he could find—the back of an envelope. These are Key's words:

"The Star-Spangled Banner"

"O say, can you see, by the dawn's early light,
What so proudly we hail'd at the twilight's last gleaming?
Whose broad stripes and bright stars, thro' the perilous fight,
O'er the ramparts we watch'd, were so gallantly streaming?
And the rockets' red glare, the bombs bursting in air,
Gave proof thro' the night that our flag was still there.
O say, does that star-spangled Banner yet wave,
O'er the Land of the free and the home of the brave?"

We usually sing only the first verse of "The Star-Spangled Banner," but there's more! The second verse speaks of Key's sighting of the flag at sunrise. The third verse praises God for saving the nation.

The actual banner Francis Scott Key so eagerly looked for measured 30 feet high by 42 feet long (about as big as a basketball court). Each stripe was two feet wide. Each star measured two feet between points. It was sewn together with 350,000 stitches. He didn't need binoculars to see it!

Francis Scott Key's poem was first titled "The Defense of Fort McHenry." But it soon became known as "The Star Spangled Banner." Congress officially declared it our national anthem in 1931. You can see the actual flag that flew from Fort McHenry at the Smithsonian Museum in Washington, D.C.

ACTIVITY: Create Kitchen Fireworks

The fireworks displays that are so common at our country's birthday celebrations remind us of the "bombs bursting in air" that we sing about in the national anthem. Next time you sing this wonderful song, you can produce your own "fireworks."

What You Need
★ Whole milk
★ Liquid dishwashing detergent
★ Food coloring
★ Cake pan

What You Do

Pour some milk into the cake pan.

Squeeze several drops of coloring in different places in the milk.

Squirt some dishwashing detergent into the milk.

Watch the colors burst into action, exploding in vivid swirls.

Just look—don't taste!

When the action slows down, add another squirt of detergent.

"AMERICA THE BEAUTIFUL"

Katharine Lee Bates wrote "America the Beautiful" in 1893 when she was 34 years old and traveling across America from her home in Massachusetts. She had visited the magnificent Niagara Falls in upstate New York, the fascinating Chicago World's Fair in Illinois, and the enormous grain fields of the Midwest. Then she found herself in Colorado, sitting at the top of Pikes Peak, one of the most beautiful mountains in the Rockies.

She was awed by the incredible scenery. She thought about the amazing sights she had seen on her trip. She began writing about the beauty of our country, the many opportunities Americans have, and her hope that God would continue to bless this nation with its ideals of freedom and equality for all.

Her poem didn't attract much attention at first. Two years passed before it was published in a church newsletter in Boston. Bostonians loved it, and soon it appeared in print all over America. Composers set it to music, trying several different melodies. But the tune Americans loved the best was an old one by Samuel Ward. It fit perfectly with the words of Bates's poem:

"O beautiful for spacious skies,
For amber waves of grain,
For purple mountain majesties
Above the fruited plain!

America! America!
God shed His grace on thee,
And crown thy good with brotherhood
From sea to shining sea!

O beautiful for pilgrim feet
Whose stern, impassioned stress
A thoroughfare for freedom beat
Across the wilderness!

America! America!
God mend thine every flaw,
Confirm thy soul in self-control,
Thy liberty in law!

O beautiful for heroes proved
In liberating strife,
Who more than self their country loved
And mercy more than life!

America! America!
May God thy gold refine

Till all success be nobleness
And every gain divine!

O beautiful for patriot dream
That sees beyond the years
Thine alabaster cities gleam
Undimmed by human tears!

America! America!
God shed His grace on thee
And crown thy good with brotherhood
From sea to shining sea!"

ACTIVITY: Be a Dictionary Detective

Pretend you're a detective, out to find the true meaning of an important, top-secret message. Write down the song "America the Beautiful" word-for-word and discover what it means.

What You Need
★ Good dictionary
★ Pencil
★ Paper

What You Do

Start writing the words to "America the Beautiful." When you come to a word you don't know the meaning of, look it up in the dictionary.

Write the meaning on the next line.

After you have done this with the entire song, take another piece of paper and write your own thoughts and ideas about the song.

THE PLEDGE OF ALLEGIANCE

In 1892, a Baptist minister named Francis Bellamy wrote a pledge, or promise, "to be true to the country he loved." The promise was this: "I pledge allegiance to my flag and the Republic for which it stands, one nation, indivisible, with liberty and justice for all."

In 1923, the National Flag Conference changed "my flag" to "the flag of the United States of America." In 1954, Congress added the words "under God" to the pledge, so today we say:

"I pledge allegiance to the flag of the United States of America.
And to the Republic for which it stands
One Nation under God, indivisible, with liberty and justice for all."

ACTIVITY: Design a Beach-Towel Banner

What You Need
- ★ Newspapers
- ★ White beach towel
- ★ Blue and red fabric paints or fabric markers
- ★ Star stencils (optional)

What You Do
Spread out newspapers in your garage. You can do this outside if it's not too windy.

Spread out your towel on top of the newspapers.

Get creative! You can decorate your towel with random stars and stripes. Or paint a line of small American flags down the middle, in a circular pattern, or as a border across the top and bottom.

Let the paint dry.

You might even want to reproduce the very first American flag on your beach towel. People will notice and will ask why there are only thirteen stars on your American flag. You can explain about the thirteen original colonies and how they became states, and why our founders chose the colors red, white, and blue.

OH, THE THINGS AMERICANS SAY

Remember Benjamin Franklin? He became a rich man through hard work. As you know, he was a great inventor. He even invented a famous saying that you've often heard: "No pain, no gain."

Well, Franklin actually said, "There are no gains without pains." He also said, "Early to bed, early to rise, makes a man healthy, wealthy, and wise." In other words, don't stay up late or sleep in—see, your parents were right!

Reverence means respect and awe; *illumination* means shining a light, or making clear; *emancipation* means setting free.

Remember John Adams? He said, "I always consider the settlement of America with reverence and wonder, as the opening of a grand scene and design in providence, for the illumination of the ignorant and the emancipation of the slavish part of mankind all over the earth."

Patrick Henry made his choice clear: "Give me liberty or give me death!"

Stephen Hopkins, a Continental Congress member from Rhode Island Colony, had an illness that made his hands shake. When he signed the Declaration of Independence, he said, "My hand trembles, but my heart does not."

James Madison, another of our founding fathers (who also served as our fourth president), delivered this meaningful mouthful: "We have staked the whole of all our political institutions upon the capacity of mankind for self-government, upon the capacity of each and all of us to govern ourselves, to control ourselves, to sustain ourselves according to the ten commandments of God."

ACTIVITY: Decorate Patriotic Flip-Flops

What You Need
- ★ One pair of white flip-flop sandals
- ★ White craft glue
- ★ Red and blue buttons

What You Do

Glue red and blue buttons across the top side of the flip-flop straps.

Let them dry a couple of hours before wearing.

All-American HOLIDAYS

Americans enjoy many holidays that are celebrated in other countries all over the world, like Christmas, Easter, and Valentine's Day. But we also observe holidays that are ours, and ours alone—national holidays to honor important people or events that have meaning to Americans. The liveliest of these is the Fourth of July, Independence Day.

The USA's birthday party is the best birthday bash ever! It brightens the sky from "sea to shining sea." The Fourth of July is our country's favorite patriotic holiday and highlights one of the most important events in American history—when leaders from the thirteen original American colonies signed the Declaration of Independence—the document that "gave birth" to the United States of America.

Colonial leaders actually voted a big fat YES to independence on July 2. But they didn't start signing the Declaration until the Fourth of July. And the signing wasn't completed until August. Even so, the Fourth was declared the official birthday of the newborn nation.

THE PENNSYLVANIA EVENING POST was the first newspaper to print the Declaration of Independence.

On July 4, 1776, bells were rung all over Philadelphia. People gathered in front of the State House, where the Declaration of Independence was read aloud publicly for the first time.

Eager messengers leapt on their horses and galloped off with copies of the new document. They spread the joyful news throughout the colonies. Everywhere the Declaration was read, Americans burst out cheering—it was party time!

Independence, yay!

Americans who lived way out in the boonies didn't know for weeks that a brand-new country had been born and that they belonged to it. As the news spread, so did lively celebrations. Men and boys fired their guns and threw their hats high in the air. Cannons boomed the good tidings. Families gathered for giant potluck picnics. They ate outside because there weren't any houses big enough to hold everyone.

But when the parties were over, Americans still had to deal with the ravages and challenges of war. For the next eight years they sacrificed much to win their freedom from Great Britain. When the war finally ended in 1783, Americans rejoiced on the Fourth of July with fireworks, parades, food, games, activities, and patriotic speeches.

It wasn't until **1941, 165 years** after that first **Fourth of July celebration, that Congress declared the Fourth an official federal holiday**—a day when government offices close so that all Americans can celebrate our independence.

When John Adams and other colonial leaders in Philadelphia voted America into existence, they knew the world would never be the same. In a letter to his wife, Adams wrote that the decision for independence "ought to be celebrated by pomp and parade, with shows, games, sports, guns, bells, bonfires, and illuminations from one end of this continent to the other." He hoped it "would become the great anniversary festival" for all Americans. And it is!

Patriotic Picnics

Over the years, picnics have become an important part of an all-American Fourth of July. So have baseball games and parades. We decorate our homes, cars, bicycles, and businesses with red, white, and blue. We even dress in red, white, and blue.

We launch fireworks from backyards, balconies, skyscrapers, mountaintops, ships, parks, and sports stadiums. We dance in the streets, tap our feet to the rhythms of marching bands, and sing "The Star-Spangled Banner" and "America the Beautiful." Some communities have "freedom" walks and runs, "liberty" bike rides, and contests with footraces, wheelbarrow races, three-legged races, sack races, egg tosses, wild pig chases, and greased pole climbing!

ACTIVITY: Fly a Liberty Wind Sock

What You Need

★ An empty, tube-shaped cardboard container, like an oatmeal box
★ Scissors
★ Red, white, and blue construction paper
★ Glue
★ Red, white, and blue crepe paper
★ Hole puncher
★ Thick yarn or string

What You Do

1. Cut out the bottom of the cardboard tube so it's open on both ends.

2. Cut a piece of red, white, or blue construction paper to wrap around the tube and then glue it around the tube to cover it completely. The tube is now red, white, or blue.

3. Cut star shapes out of construction paper in colors different from the tube.

4. Glue the stars onto the tube.

5. Cut red, white, and blue streamers from the crepe paper and glue them to one end of the tube (this will be the bottom end).

What You Do Next

1. On the other end of the tube (the top end), punch a hole one half inch from the top end of the tube. Now punch a second hole exactly opposite across from the first hole. Now punch a third hole on the side of the tube, halfway between the first and second holes. Punch the fourth and final hole directly opposite the third hole.

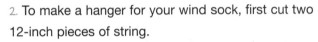

2. To make a hanger for your wind sock, first cut two 12-inch pieces of string.

3. Tie a large knot at the end of one of the 12-inch pieces of string. Thread the other end from inside the tube through one of the holes. The knot inside will keep it from coming all the way through.

4. Then thread the piece of string through the hole on the opposite side of the tube. Thread it in from the outside so that it is identical to the first side. Tie a knot from the inside. You should now have a string handle.

5. Do the same thing with the other piece of string and the two remaining holes.

6. Now tie a longer piece of string to the top middle of the two string "handles." Use this piece of string to hang the wind sock from a window, a fence post, or porch.

The westernmost Fourth of July celebration takes place in Hawaii, thousands of miles west of the North American continent where the other 49 states are located.

Three of our presidents have died on our country's birthday—John Adams, Thomas Jefferson (both in 1826), and James Monroe (in 1831).

Washington, D.C., puts on a spectacular fireworks display on the Capitol lawn—guaranteed to light up the sky, rattle the windows, and make the crowds ooh and aah! If you can't make it to D.C. to attend the fireworks and the National Independence Day Parade on Constitution Avenue, you can watch both on television. Or, better yet, go outside and enjoy your town's celebration.

★ **EXTRA** ★

Many American newspapers print the full text of the Declaration of Independence on the Fourth of July.

In Boston, you might see the USS *John F. Kennedy*, a battleship, cruise into Boston Harbor with Old Glory flying high. The Boston Symphony broadcasts stirring patriotic music.

FAVORITE FOURTH OF JULY FOODS

Food is at the heart of any really good Fourth of July party. A chilled watermelon wedge, salty corn on the cob soaked with butter, chicken and ribs barbecued on the grill, creamy homemade ice cream—take away our favorite foods and this holiday would lose a lot of its "flavor"!

Take, for instance, watermelon. (But don't take my piece!) Watermelon is so wonderfully refreshing because it's about 93 percent water! Most people picture the insides of a watermelon as juicy and red with bunches of seeds. But watermelon insides also come in white, yellow, and orange—and some have no seeds at all. Besides being delicious, watermelon is good for you, containing vitamins C and A, and potassium, a mineral you can't live without.

ACTIVITY: Make a Watermelon Bowl Fruit Salad

What You Need

★ A ripe watermelon

★ A melon scoop or baller

★ An assortment of your favorite fruits

★ A fresh lime (optional)

★ An adult assistant

What You Do

Wash your hands with soap. Then wash the outside of the watermelon well. Ask your adult assistant to cut the watermelon in half, lengthwise.

Scoop all the watermelon out of the rind and set it aside in a large container.

Cut additional fruits like strawberries, pineapple, cantaloupe, honeydew, and bananas into bite-size pieces. Add blueberries and grapes, if you like.

Mix all the fruit together and place in the watermelon "bowl."

Squeeze the juice from a fresh lime across the top of the fruit, if desired.

Cover the watermelon bowl with plastic wrap and chill till ready to serve.

YUM!

Many Americans still have ties to the Old Country and its customs, whether those ties are recent or go back hundreds of years. Over the years, some of the Old Country traditions—especially ethnic foods—have mixed with American Fourth of July traditions.

In Ohio, for example, where a lot of people's grandparents, great-grandparents, and great-great-grandparents came from Germany, the Fourth is not the Fourth without German potato salad. In El Paso, Texas, right across the border from Mexico, you'll find tasty tamales on the table. In Boston, one of America's oldest sea harbors, it's chowder, chowder, and more chowder—there's an annual Fourth of July contest where Bostonians chow down thousands of gallons of different types of seafood chowder right along the waterfront.

FIREWORKS FACTS

Americans celebrate with about $130 million of fireworks a year! We spend more than $50 million each year for American flags. You already know all about flags. Here's the scoop on fireworks:

Fireworks are made with gunpowder and other ingredients that explode into colorful sparks when they're lit. Fireworks that explode with a loud noise but no colorful sparks are called firecrackers.

EVERY YEAR AMERICANS ARE INJURED, AND EVEN DIE, IN ACCIDENTS WITH FIRE-WORKS. So, you must have an adult's supervision when you use fireworks. In fact, let the grown-ups deal with the fireworks and you just sit back and enjoy the show.

In most states it's against the law for nonprofessionals to set off fireworks. Kids should NEVER handle fireworks. Like Uncle Sam says, this means YOU!

SKYROCKETS

Skyrockets are so hot they're cool. Here's how they work: A fuse sticks out from the rear of a rocket. The fuse is usually made of twisted paper soaked in a substance that will catch fire easily. The "body" of the rocket is made of a cardboard tube that contains two separate charges (portions) of gunpowder. After the fuse is lit, it burns its way to the body and ignites the first charge of gunpowder, which is called coarse gunpowder.

When the coarse gunpowder ignites, it forms powerful gasses that explode out the end of the paper tube. The force of the explosion launches the rocket skyward. As the rocket reaches its highest point (when it runs out of gasses), the last bit of coarse gunpowder ignites the second charge of fine gunpowder. The fine gunpowder burns to the "nose" of the rocket, igniting a bunch of small firecrackers packed inside it. BOOOOOOM!

MORE USA HOLIDAYS

Fortunately, Independence Day is not the only all-American holiday! From the beginning of the year to the end, here are some more made-in-the-USA holidays.

 ## Martin Luther King Day
January—Third Monday

Martin Luther King Jr. is America's most famous civil rights leader. Civil rights are the privileges the United States Constitution guarantees each and every American citizen—liberty, equality, and justice, for example.

Older Americans feel shame when they remember that less than fifty years ago in our country black people were not allowed to go to the same schools, eat at the same restaurants, stay at the same hotels, or sit alongside white people on busses and trains. King, an African American, spent his life fighting for equal treatment for Americans of all races.

King was a man of peace. He asked African Americans to use peaceful ways to try to change these inequalities. He led peaceful marches all over America to get people to pay attention to his message of true freedom for all Americans.

His most famous speech is called the "I Have a Dream" speech because he spoke of his hopes and dreams for a better America:

"I have a dream that one day on the red hills of Georgia the sons of former slaves and the sons of former slaveowners will be able to sit down together at a table of brotherhood.

"I have a dream that my four children will one day live in a nation where they will not be judged by the color of their skin but by the content of their character.

Liberty = Freedom
Equality = The same rights and privileges for all Americans
Justice = Fair and honest treatment

"I have a dream that one day . . . little black boys and black girls will be able to join hands with little white boys and white girls and walk together as sisters and brothers."

Change has come slowly. It has often seemed to African Americans that conditions would never improve, but King's words are powerful: "I say to you today, my friends, that even though we face the difficulties of today and tomorrow, I still have a dream. I have a dream that one day this nation will rise up and live out the true meaning of its creed—'We hold these truths to be self-evident, that all men are created equal.'"

Martin Luther King Jr. Day was officially established in 1983. On the third Monday in January, schools, banks, and government offices (like the post office) close. King's "I Have a Dream" speech is reprinted in newspapers and replayed on radio and television stations, reminding Americans that what King had to say is just as important today as it was then—that it is up to ALL of us to make America a place where everyone is treated with respect, and where every single person gets the same chance to do and be their very best.

ACTIVITY: Create a King Day Patriotic Wreath

What You Need

★ Paper plate
★ Red, white, and blue construction paper

★ Scissors
★ Glue

What You Do

Cut a hole from the center of the paper plate so it looks like a donut. Leave about 2 inches of plate around the outside. Throw away the middle cut-out part.

Cut star shapes from blue, red, and white construction paper.

Write "I Have a Dream" on some of the stars. Write some of the things King dreamed about on the others.

Glue the stars onto the paper plate.

Presidents' Day
February—third Monday

The February birthdays of our most famous presidents, George Washington and Abraham Lincoln, used to be celebrated as two separate holidays. Washington is most remembered for helping "invent" our country, being a brave general, and being America's first president. Lincoln is most remembered for guiding America through the Civil War and for helping our country heal afterwards.

Lincoln was a common man, from a poor family, who had experienced many hardships. His honesty, along with his determination to always do the right thing, made him a wise and strong leader. People called him Honest Abe.

He is famous for the Gettysburg Address, a speech that begins: "Fourscore and seven years ago our fathers brought forth on this continent a new nation, conceived in liberty and dedicated to the proposition that all men are created equal."

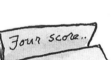

His speech ends with, " . . . this nation, under God, shall have a new birth of freedom—and that the government of the people, by the people, shall not perish from the earth."

ENDING SLAVERY

The Civil War ended slavery in the United States. Before that, wealthy farmers in the southern states could own African Americans as slaves. Most Northerners thought slavery was wrong and should be against the law. Many Southerners disagreed and decided to quit the United States and become a separate country rather than set the slaves free. Abraham Lincoln wouldn't let them—the most important goal of his presidency was to end slavery and to reunite the northern and southern states. Only then could America really and truly be a free country.

Lincoln said, "As I would not be a Slave so I would not be a Master. This idea expresses my idea of democracy—whatever differs from this, to the extent of the difference, is no democracy."

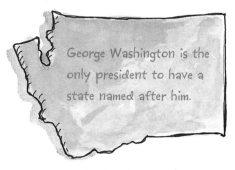

George Washington is the only president to have a state named after him.

In 1971, the two presidential birthday celebrations were combined and expanded to honor ALL Americans who have held one of the hardest but greatest jobs in the world—president of the United States.

Why is it so hard to be president? Because our country is the most powerful nation in the world. That means we have a huge responsibility as a world leader. The decisions our country's government makes affect the lives of people all over the world. Also, we are a very diverse country—that means Americans are of many different races and religions and have many different ideas about how things should be done. The president has to represent ALL of us.

ACTIVITY: Make a Lincoln Penny Necklace

What You Need

★ Construction paper (red, white, and blue)
★ Scissors
★ Tape measure or ruler
★ White glue or glue stick

★ A Lincoln penny
★ Hole puncher
★ Red, white, or blue yarn

What You Do

Cut out a red star, measuring about 1¼ inches across

Cut out a white star, 1 inch across

Cut out a blue star, ¾ inch across

Glue the white star onto the red star, and the blue star onto the white star.

Glue a Lincoln penny on top of the blue star with the top point of the star facing up. Make sure Lincoln's face is showing and is right side up.

Punch a hole through the top of the star point above Lincoln's profile.

Thread a piece of red, white, or blue yarn through the hole and tie the ends together. Make sure the yarn is long enough for you to slip the necklace over your head.

Memorial Day

May 30

The first Memorial Day celebration took place in 1866, in Waterloo, New York, when the Civil War was finally over. A Waterloo pharmacist named Henry Welles came up with the idea of honoring local soldiers who had died in the war by decorating their graves.

Henry and other townspeople decided to set aside a day in May to plant flowers and place wreaths and crosses on the graves of their sons, brothers, fathers, friends, and neighbors who had died in the war. (It was a terrible war and almost everyone had lost someone they loved.) All over Waterloo, flags were flown at half-mast. Black streamers decorated many of the businesses and homes.

One year later, the townspeople got together for a bigger and better repeat performance, this time adding a parade with veterans (soldiers who had survived the Civil War) marching alongside a band playing military music. There were ceremonies with speeches and prayers at all three of the town's cemeteries.

"Let every nation know, whether it wishes us well or ill, that we shall pay any price, bear any burden, meet any hardship, support any friend, oppose any foe, to assure the survival and success of liberty."
—President John F. Kennedy

Other towns and cities latched onto Waterloo's idea. The next year "Decoration Day," as it was called, was celebrated all across America. All because Henry Welles was inspired to honor American soldiers and decided to do something about it!

But it wasn't official for another hundred years. In 1971, Congress changed the name to Memorial Day and made it a national holiday. Flags are still flown high and proud and Americans still visit war memorials and the cemeteries where soldiers are buried, to leave flowers and flags and other remembrances on their graves.

It's a small way of saying a big "thank-you" to the many Americans who have died while protecting our nation.

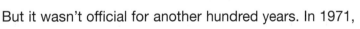

Memorial Day is officially on May 30, but it's celebrated on the closest Monday to the 30th so that businesses and schools can enjoy a three-day weekend. Many people consider this weekend the beginning of summer, even though summer doesn't technically start until later on in June.

Flag Day

June 14

American flags seem to be everywhere on Flag Day, when it's "hats off" to Old Glory. It's not really the flag we celebrate—it's what the flag stands for. By showing respect for our flag we're showing respect for our nation.

You already know that in 1777 the Continental Congress chose the red, white, and blue stars and stripes for our flag. You might not know that it wasn't until 1877, on the hundred-year anniversary of our flag, that Congress declared that American flags should be flown on all government buildings.

Labor Day

September—first Monday

Even though summer is coming to a close, Labor Day is party time! Because it's on a Monday, an ordinary, two-day weekend turns into a three-day weekend—which means an extra day to picnic, go to the lake, camp—to whoop it up with one last holiday hurrah before saying so-long to summer for another year. (Just as Memorial Day unofficially "ushers in" summer, Labor Day unofficially ushers it out.)

But why is it called Labor Day when most Americans play instead of work? America was built on the labor (another word for hard work) of laborers (workers). On Labor Day we honor the many jobs American workers do. America wouldn't even exist without the contributions of millions and millions of hardworking Americans, from the very beginning of our nation's history.

There was a time, though, when many American workers had to put up with unsafe conditions and very low pay. On their own, they had no power to change things. So they joined together into groups of workers called labor unions. Together they had more power and could demand better working conditions and better pay.

The first Labor Day celebration took place in New York in 1882, when a labor union organized a parade and picnic to celebrate its power and unity. More than ten thousand workers took a day off from work to march through New York City. Their idea was contagious and workers elsewhere followed their example. In 1894, Labor Day became an official national holiday (meaning the whole country celebrated it).

Nowadays, Canada, as well as many other countries, has also set aside a day to honor workers.

 ## Columbus Day
October—second Monday

Back in the 1400s, spices, fabrics, and other products from China, India, and other Asian countries were very popular in Europe. Europeans paid lots of money for them, which meant sea captains could get rich by sailing to Asia and bringing back the goods Europeans wanted. But it was a long and dangerous trip and could take years.

An Italian sea captain and explorer named Christopher Columbus had an idea for a short-cut. Shorter trips, more often, would equal more money. Columbus had read lots of geography books and had studied maps of the world. He came to the conclusion that the world was round, not flat, as many people then still believed. He was convinced he'd find a shorter route by traveling west instead of east. He believed that he could sail a circle right around the world to India. It was risky business—if the world turned out to be flat after all, he'd be in big trouble!

He talked Spain's king and queen into providing him with ninety men and three ships, the *Niña*, the *Pinta*, and the *Santa Maria*. Away they sailed, west across the Atlantic Ocean, headed straight for India—or so Columbus thought. Instead, on October 12, 1492, they bumped right into a brand-new world (part of it anyway)—the Bahama Islands, to be more exact. Later on, Columbus made second and third trips to America, bringing people and horses to live in America.

Fast forward three hundred years to 1792, when New York City held a ceremony in honor of the three hundredth anniversary of Columbus landing in America. The "discovery" of America had turned out to be one of the most important events in the history of the world. Before that, Europeans didn't even know there was a North America—much less a South America. News of a New World eventually led to the greatest migration, or movement, of people ever—a migration that continues today.

Fans of Columbus had to make do with that first celebration in 1792 for quite a while, because a lot of years went by before the next celebration, on October 12, 1866. That one was organized by New York's Italian American population, who wanted the whole country to know how proud they were of the most famous Italian in American history! Three years later, Italian Americans in San Francisco, California, followed New York's example with their own October 12 celebration. They get the credit for coming up with the name "Columbus Day."

As the years passed, the celebrations became an annual October event throughout the country, and President Franklin Roosevelt proclaimed it an official holiday in 1937. In 1968, it became a federal holiday. That year the date for Columbus Day was changed to the second Monday in October, making a three-day weekend. (We all love those three-day weekends!)

Nowadays Columbus Day is celebrated in all but nine of our states and also in some parts of Canada, Central and South America, and even Europe. In some states it's called Discovery Day or Landing Day. New York City has a huge Columbus Day parade.

Veterans' Day
November 11

Here's your chance to honor all Americans who have served (or are serving) in any of our country's armed forces—including the Marines, the Navy, the Air Force, the Army, and the Coast Guard. Even when our country is at peace, the armed services are working hard, ready to defend us if they need to.

ACTIVITY: Support Our Troops

What You Need
What You Do

★ Pencil or pen
★ Paper
★ Envelope

★ Stamp
★ Computer
★ Internet access

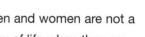

Write a letter of thanks to someone in one of our armed forces. Many of these men and women are not a lot older than you are. They miss their families, their homes, and the American way of life when they are serving in far-off countries. Tell them how much you appreciate them.

Use a computer to log on to www.anysoldier.com to find out where to send your letter.

Thanksgiving Day
November—fourth Thursday

Thanksgiving, the very first American holiday in 1621, came about when the Pilgrims said a great big THANK-YOU for their first good American harvest. They believed God had blessed them in the new country and they wanted to make a special point of thanking him and the Native Americans who helped them settle in the new land.

They feasted on deer meat, ocean fish, and roasted birds—probably turkeys. They also prepared berries and other fruits. Boiled pumpkin was served, but pumpkin pie was not an option because there was a shortage of flour. Like all good parties, that first Thanksgiving included games and races.

Can someone please passeth the boiled pumpkin?

More than 150 years passed before Thanksgiving was celebrated among all thirteen colonies. And it was almost another hundred years before it became an annual (yearly) national holiday. That happened after a magazine editor named Sarah Hale wrote and published several articles proposing that Thanksgiving be made a national holiday. President Lincoln liked her idea and made it official in 1863, setting aside the last Thursday in November.

ACTIVITY: Write a "Thankful" List

Before you dig into your Thanksgiving feast, pause to be thankful for the country we live in and the many freedoms and opportunities we have as Americans!

What You Need

★ Paper

★ Pencil or pen

What You Do

Write down ten things you're thankful for.

Read your list aloud to the family and friends you celebrate with.

You can start an annual tradition this way. Each year you can read the list from the year before. It will be like a diary, reminding you of what was on your mind and in your heart on other Thanksgivings!

"America lives in the heart of every man who wishes to find a region where he will be free to work out his destiny as he chooses."
—President Woodrow Wilson

Freedom and democracy are alive and well in the USA.

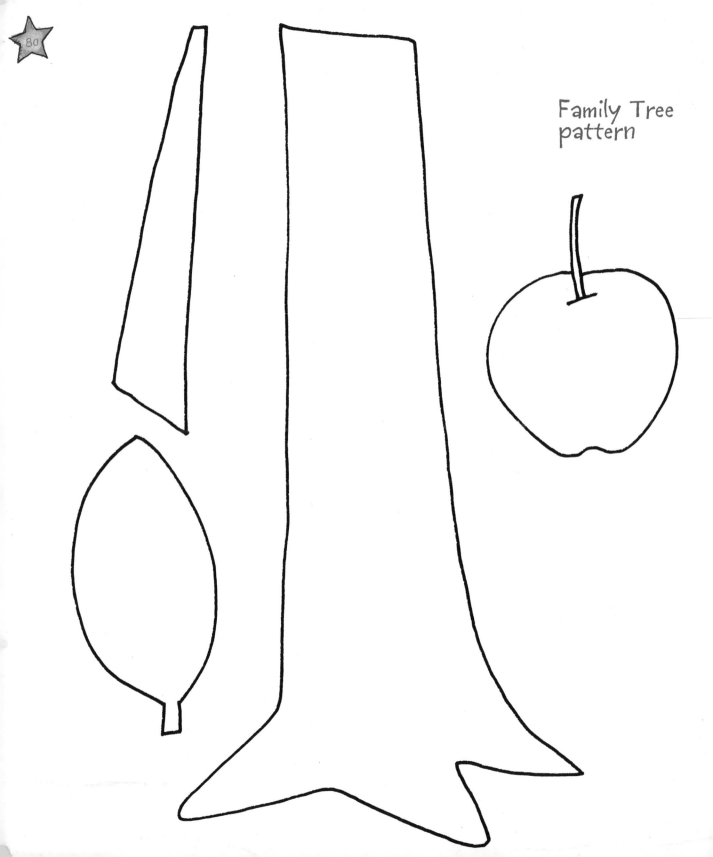

Family Tree
pattern

SPLENDID SAMPLERS

to Cross-Stitch

SPLENDID SAMPLERS

to Cross-Stitch

■■■■■

35 Original Projects

Chris Rankin

Sterling Publishing Co., Inc.   New York
A Sterling/Lark Book

Editor: Bobbe Needham
Art Director: Chris Bryant
Production: Elaine Thompson
English Translation: Networks, Inc., and Irene Selent
Editorial Assistance: Stephanie Johnston and Ethan Skemp

Library of Congress Cataloging-in-Publication Data
Rankin, Chris.
    Splendid samplers to cross-stitch : 35 original projects / Chris Rankin.
       p.   cm.
    "A Sterling/Lark book."
    Includes index.
    ISBN 0-8069-3164-7
    1. Needlework--Patterns.   2. Samplers.   I. Title.
TT753.R36   1995
746.44'2041--dc20   95-11548
                                                       CIP

10 9 8 7 6 5 4 3 2 1

A Sterling/Lark Book

First paperback edition published in 1996 by
   Sterling Publishing Company, Inc.
   387 Park Avenue South, New York, N.Y. 10016

Produced by Altamont Press, Inc.
   50 College Street, Asheville, NC 28801

Pages 46, 47, 56, 92-93: Photos and original instructions
© Libelle Special/Uitgeverij Spaarnestad, Haarlem, Holland

Other projects and original instructions
© Ariadne/Spaarnestad, Utrecht, Holland

English translation © 1995 by Altamont Press

Distributed in Canada by Sterling Publishing
   c/o Canadian Manda Group, One Atlantic Avenue, Suite 105
   Toronto, Ontario, Canada M6K 3E7

Distributed in Great Britain and Europe by Cassell PLC
   Wellington House, 125 Strand, London WC2R 0BB, England

Distributed in Australia by Capricorn Link (Australia) Pty Ltd.
   P.O. Box 6651, Baulkham Hills, Business Centre, NSW 2153, Australia

Printed in Hong Kong
All rights reserved

Sterling ISBN 0-8069-3164-7 Trade
             0-8069-3165-5 Paper

Contents

Introduction

WHAT IS IT ABOUT SAMPLERS? I've always been drawn to them. Hanging in antique stores, on a friend's wall, or in a historic home, those pictures painted with thread, those mottos and alphabets, names and dates written with tiny stitches speak to me of time and care and artistry.

Maybe it's the history. Maybe it's knowing that children and women (mostly) have been stitching samplers for centuries. Maybe it's imagining ten-year-old girls sitting in a row in a schoolroom in seventeenth-century England or eighteenth-century Connecticut, poking their needles in and out of somewhat grimy, unevenly woven linen under a schoolmistress's watchful eye.

Twelve-year-old Elizabeth Boulton stitched this sampler in silk on wool in early nineteenth-century England. Reproduced with permission, Division of Textiles, National Museum of American History, Smithsonian Institution.

Starting Out

HERE'S the secret to a beautiful cross-stitched sampler: work all the upper crossing stitches in the same direction—say, from the lower left to the upper right of the x. Crossing the stitches in different directions makes the light reflect off them differently and makes them look uneven. Break this rule to emphasize a part of the design—switch the direction of your upper stitches in that area.

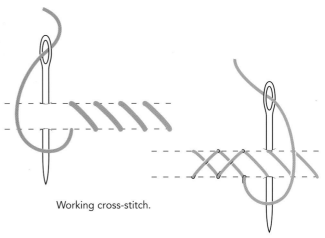

Working cross-stitch.

To save time and thread, work back and forth across a motif in rows, slanting all the lower threads one way as you stitch in one direction and the upper threads the other way on the return trip, as shown in the two illustrations.

For diagonal rows of stitches, scattered individual stitches, or single stitches of one color, most cross-stitchers find that completing one stitch at a time works best.

Deciding on Fabrics

TO WORK a sampler, you have to be able to count the threads of your fabric, because you make each cross-stitch over an intersection of those threads. Typical project directions in the book, for example, tell you to "cross-stitch the motif using two strands of floss over two threads" of fabric for each stitch.

Today's even-weave fabrics, with the same number of warp and weft threads per inch or per centimeter, help ensure you even cross-stitches. Although any even-weave fabric will work, one that a veteran cross-stitcher finds challenging and satisfying might discourage a beginner. Close weaves—that is, those with more threads to the inch—mean more difficult and exacting needlework. The paragraph on materials for each project tells you what fabric appears in the pictured example, including its thread count—for instance, "ecru linen with 25 threads per inch (10 per cm)."

The samplers in the book call for popular and easy-to-find even-weave fabrics: linen, Aida, and Hardanger. Probably the most expensive of these, linen is both beautiful and durable and comes in weaves from coarse to fine. Two popular cottons are Aida cloth, which is 100 percent cotton and has between eleven and twenty-two threads per inch, and Hardanger cloth, a cotton blend that resists fraying, with twenty-five or twenty-seven threads to the inch.

Using the Charts

EACH sampler in the book has an accompanying chart—a graph of the finished embroidery. Each symbol on the chart represents one cross-stitch, and the key to the chart lists a different color of floss for each symbol.

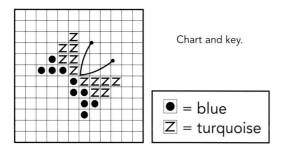

Chart and key.

● = blue
Z = turquoise

On the chart for the butterfly shown here, for instance, the dots stand for blue and the z's for turquoise. To stitch the butterfly, on the bottom row you make one blue stitch; on the second row, another blue stitch above it and one to the right; on the third row, working from left to right, two blue stitches, then two turquoise stitches, and so on.

To keep your place on the chart, you might move a small ruler or index card down the rows as you work or pencil through each row as you complete it.

Before you begin a sampler, you'll want to be sure your finished embroidery will end up in the middle of the fabric. Matching the center of the motif (that is, the center of the chart) to the center of your fabric ensures that your embroidery won't run off one side. To find the center of the fabric, fold the fabric end to end, then side to side. Mark both centerlines with tailor's chalk, straight pins, or basting thread.

You can then count the stitches on the chart from this central point to each edge, translate this figure onto your fabric in terms of threads per stitch, and figure out where the edges of your embroidery will fall. Say you count 100 stitches (squares) on the chart from the center to the right-hand edge, and the directions call for making each stitch over two threads of fabric. You can figure the right-hand edge of your embroidery will fall 200 threads to the right of the centerline on your fabric.

Selecting Needles, Floss, and Hoops

THE LARGE eyes and blunt points of tapestry needles make them ideal for cross-stitching, for they hold multiple strands of floss and push the fabric fibers apart without splitting threads or previous stitches. A packet of assorted sizes (say, #20 to #24) will work for most fabrics. The higher the number, the smaller the needle. Coarser fabrics call for larger needles, finer fabrics for smaller. For example, a #24 needle works well for eleven-count Aida cloth—that is, for any fabric with eleven threads per inch (4.5 per cm).

The six-strand cotton embroidery floss cross-stitchers use comes in almost every conceivable color. Each skein runs approximately nine yards (8.2 m). For each sampler in the book, the key to the chart supplies, along with each color, the corresponding product number for two widely available brands of floss, DMC and Anchor. (You may of course substitute another brand—or even rewrite the color key.) When the pictured samplers have been worked in some other thread, that is noted and its color numbers listed.

Many cross-stitchers find that embroidery hoops slow them down or distort stitches, and leaving work in a hoop even overnight may permanently stretch the fabric. Ironing the finished sampler takes care of any fabric creases or unevenness of tension in the stitches. If you feel that a hoop helps keep your stitching even, look for a two-ring wood or plastic hoop that you can adjust with a screw on the outer ring.

Sampler Tip
BLEEDING FLOSS

If you're unsure whether a particular color of floss will bleed (that is, whether the color will run), wash the skein in plenty of lukewarm water. If it bleeds, rinse it with cold water until the water runs clear. Don't wring it out. Fold it in a towel and press out the moisture, then let it dry.

Making a Floss Caddy

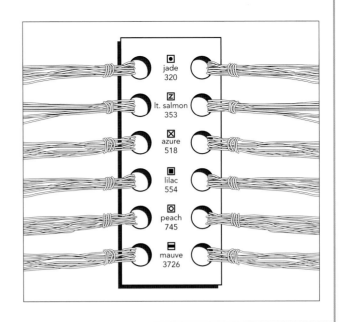

ESPECIALLY when your project calls for many colors of floss, you may yearn for a way to organize all those skeins. Craft or fabric shops offer a variety of organizers, but you can easily make one, as shown here.

Punch holes along the sides of a stiff card or piece of cardboard. Then cut one skein of the floss called for in your project to lengths of about fourteen to twenty-four inches (36 to 62 cm) each. Hold one end of the lengths together and thread this through a hole in the cardboard, as shown here. Label each skein with its symbol on the key to the project chart, its brand, and its shade number.

Working Cross-Stitch

A SHORT length of floss works best for cross-stitching— about fourteen to twenty-four inches (36 to 62 cm).

~ THE FABRIC ~

To keep your fabric from fraying as you work at your embroidery, you need to finish the raw edges in one of several ways. For closely woven fabric, you can finish the edges with a row of machine or hand zigzag stitches. For most fabrics, you can simply turn over a narrow hem and stitch it by hand or machine. For canvas, fold masking tape around the edges or fold cotton binding over them and stitch it down firmly.

~ THE FIRST STITCH ~

Especially in looser fabric weaves, you can see that a larger opening occurs between every second thread. To make your stitch counting much easier, make your first stitch next to the vertical thread with the larger opening.

~ NEW THREAD ~

Cross-stitchers use two methods for anchoring the first stitch of a project or of a new area: leaving a tail and looping. In the first method, you leave a one-inch (2.5 cm) tail of floss dangling free at the back, then catch this tail under the next few stitches, as shown in the illustration.

The loop method works anytime you are sewing with an even number of strands of floss (the directions for each sampler specify how many strands of floss to use). For example, if the directions call for two strands of floss, cut one strand that is twice as long as the length you want to stitch with. Fold it in half and thread the needle with the two ends together, leaving a loop at the other end. Come up from the back of your fabric and make the first half cross. When you pass the needle to the back again, run it through the loop before coming up to complete the cross-stitch.

Once your sampler is under way, start new strands by running your needle under a few already worked stitches on the back of the design, then come up on the right side to begin stitching.

Avoid carrying floss across the back of an open area of light fabric for more than five squares. Dark threads especially will show through.

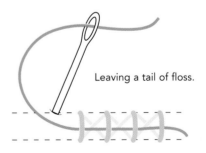

Leaving a tail of floss.

~ COLOR PLAN ~

To conserve floss, plan ahead with colors. For instance, you may stitch a turquoise flower and see that you will need turquoise again in a nearby bud. Rather than clipping off your thread and starting a new one with every color change, after you stitch the flower carry the long remaining turquoise strand along the back of your work to an out-of-the-way spot on the fabric, pull it through to the front, and take the needle off, as shown in the illustration of the vase. Continue stitching the other

Floss color planning.

colors called for in the design. When you reach the turquoise bud, pull the dangling strand through to the back of the work, rethread it, and travel on the wrong side to the bud, weaving through the backs of your newly embroidered stitches.

~ THE LAST STITCH ~

When you finish a color or strand, run the last inch or so of floss under a few stitches on the back of the sampler so no loose end shows. Snip off any excess.

When you're not embroidering, remove your needle (and hoop, if you use one) from the fabric—both leave rust marks.

Using Other Stitches

MOST projects in the book suggest that you embroider around the figures in your finished sampler with an outline stitch; some also call for a smattering of other common embroidery stitches. These are described and pictured in the stitches appendix.

Changing Sizes

TO VARY the finished size of a sampler, make your cross-stitches larger or smaller—that is, cross more or fewer threads with each stitch than the instructions call for. You'll also have to refigure the amount of fabric you'll need.

If you decide to use a different fabric or to design your own project, plan your stitch size based on the effect you want. On a fabric with fewer (thus, thicker) threads per inch, crossing two threads for each stitch gives you good-sized stitches. On a fine-woven fabric that has more threads per inch, crossing two threads results in tiny, fine stitches.

Something else to keep in mind: the more threads of fabric you cross with one stitch, the less solid the mass of color that will result, because more fabric will show behind the stitches. Also, the more strands of floss you use, the thicker and bolder the stitch. In general, stitches look best when they fill the holes of the fabric but still retain the clarity of the cross.

Choosing Colors

WHEN it comes to choosing colors for your sampler, you are the king or queen of the realm. Taste, personal preference, decor, mood, time of day—anything you choose can govern the colors of your cross-stitch project. Each sampler chart in this book comes with a color key that reflects the floss colors used in the pictured projects, but feel free to design your own palette. A color tip: When choosing floss, lay it over the fabric you will use under natural light.

Changing Letters and Numbers

YOU will nearly always want to substitute other names and dates for the ones pictured on the samplers here (except perhaps for the historic samplers). Let's say you want one line of your sampler to read "April 2, 1996," as shown here. On the original project chart:

1. Count across to find the cross-stitches allowed on each line (in this theoretical case, 82 are allowed).
2. Choose an alphabet size and style from another sampler or design your own. Count the number of spaces allowed between each letter in a word (we'll say 2), between each number in a date (2), and between each complete word or date (4).
3. If you want to include commas, periods, or hyphens, count the spaces between a word or date and a mark of punctuation (in this case, 2).

4. To make your own chart on graph paper, first mark the beginning and end points of the spaces allowed on a line of your project. In this example, we have 82 spaces to work with. Divide by two to find the center point on the chart (in this case, 41). Add up the spaces between letters and words (here, they total 24).

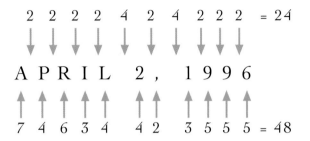

5. Add up the spaces required for each letter and number in your phrase (here, 48). Add this figure to the total of spaces in step 4: 48 + 24 = 72. We have a fit, with 5 squares of space left on each side (82-72=10).

If you find you have too much extra space, you can repeat symbols from elsewhere in the piece. To shrink lines you can abbreviate words, substitute initials for names, and so on.

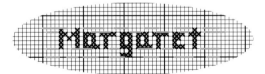

To avoid frustration, use guidelines for names, dates, and borders, as shown in the "Margaret" illustration here:

frame tricky sections of your motif by basting straight lines with bright-colored single strands of floss. When you finish cross-stitching that area, remove the basting.

Antiquing

TO GIVE your sampler an antique look, wet white or ivory linen in plain water, then soak it in strong, cold tea for about ten minutes, stirring occasionally (the fabric will dry a shade lighter). Hot tea will produce a lighter shade, cold coffee a darker one. To set the color so it won't streak if you wash it later, add a teaspoon of alum, available at drugstores. Allow the piece to drip dry, and iron before cross-stitching.

Aging works just as well for a sampler you have already embroidered, as long as the thread is color fast.

Washing and Pressing

IF YOUR finished sampler needs washing and the fabric and floss are washable, launder it like any other delicate item: slosh gently in lukewarm water and mild soap, then rinse. Depending on the fabric, either (1) roll the sampler in a towel to blot up excess moisture, then hang or lay flat to dry, or (2) machine dry it, removing it from the dryer while it is still slightly damp.

To iron out wrinkles and unevenness, cover your ironing board with a towel, then a soft cloth—ironing on a towel helps push the stitches out from the fabric, rather than flattening them down. Place your sampler face down on the cloth and cover it with another soft cloth, dampened if your piece is dry. Press lightly with a fairly hot iron. Lay the sampler flat until it dries completely.

Sampler Tip
FRAMING AND CARE

- Like a lot of us, fabrics prefer to breathe—it lengthens their life. When you frame your sampler or have it framed, try to resist covering it with glass or plastic. Just frame it.

- For storage, wrap your framed sampler in a clean pillowcase (not plastic) and set it at a slight tilt in an airy space.

- Hang your sampler away from direct sunlight, working fireplaces, or crowded kitchens—sunlight will fade it, and soot, smoke, and kitchen grease will discolor it.

Country Garden Sampler

FROM AN 1800S SAMPLER,
WHOSE MAKER LATER REMOVED THE DATE:

*"That which fragrance is to the rose,
modesty is to youth and beauty
Sharpsburg MD 18—
Eliza Ann Showmans work done
in the 14 year of her age April 22"*

FINISHED MEASUREMENTS

16-1/2 x 22-1/4 in. (42 x 57 cm)

EMBROIDERY MEASUREMENTS

12-3/4 x 19 in. (33 x 49 cm)

MATERIALS

23-1/2 x 29-1/4 in. (60 x 75 cm) of linen with 25 threads per inch (10 per cm); embroidery floss as indicated on the key to the chart plus light topaz #725 or #305; frame (optional).

DIRECTIONS

Mark the horizontal and vertical center of the fabric with basting thread, then cross-stitch according to the chart using two strands of floss over two threads of linen for each stitch.

Embroider in outline stitch over completed cross-stitch using one strand of floss:

- very dark fawn #632 or #936 in and around the tan and medium light copper pots;
- and in and around the remaining pots, the column, the bench, the wheelbarrow, the watering can, and the birds with charcoal #3799 or #236.

Embroider the remaining outline stitches in the same color as the cross-stitches or one shade darker.

Make a French knot at the centers of the flowers where indicated by black circles: in the flowers in the small pot at upper right in light pink #818 or #23; in the flowers in the pot under the arch in light grape #341 or #117; and in the pots to the left and the far right of the column in light topaz #725 or #305.

At the bottom of the sampler, make a French knot at the centers of the tall flowers at the far left in light topaz #725 or #305; in the green flowers in the small pots to the left in grape #340 or #118; and in the pine-colored flowers to the right in a mix of these two colors.

Use two strands of medium light loden green floss #3053 or #261 to embroider the flower stems and the grass next to the pots in stem stitch.

Using three strands and a daisy stitch, embroider the flower petals in the pot left of the column with grape #340 or #118, and the flower petals in the lower left pot with light blue #3755 or #140.

KEY TO CHART

		DMC	Anchor
◗	= gray	318	399
◢	= grape	340	118
⟋	= light grape	341	117
⊘	= turf	371	854
＝	= light turf	372	853
H	= tan	437	362
◣	= dark fog	451	233
◖	= pine	502	876
⟋	= light pine	503	875
⟡	= light jade	504	213
⊠	= med. light gray green	523	859
N	= light violet	553	98
L	= lilac	554	96
■	= very dark fawn	632	936
▢	= medium linen	642	392
•	= very light ecru	712	926
⟍	= light tan	738	361
＝	= medium light copper	758	882
∴	= silver	762	234
⟋	= light pink	818	23
⎮	= medium glacier blue	827	159
⚊	= denim blue	932	920
⦂	= copper	945	881
⊠	= medium light green	987	244
◿	= medium lime	989	242
⟋	= linen	3033	391
◡	= very light turf	3047	852
◣	= medium loden green	3052	262
⊠	= med. light loden green	3053	261
⋁	= medium copper	3064	883
◣	= dark loden green	3362	263
▽	= light loden green	3364	260
+	= medium pink	3716	25
⊠	= light blue	3755	140
◉	= charcoal	3799	236

Alphabets in Blue Sampler

FROM A 1630 SAMPLER:

"Caty Langdon is my name
And with my needle I rought the same
And if my skil had been better
I would have mended every letter."

FRAMED MEASUREMENTS

15-1/4 x 18 in. (39 x 46 cm)

EMBROIDERY MEASUREMENTS

12 x 15 in. (31 x 38.5 cm)

MATERIALS

23-1/2 x 25-1/4 in. (60 x 65 cm) of white linen with 26 threads per inch (10 to 11 per cm); embroidery floss as indicated on the key to the chart; a frame 15-1/4 x 18 in. (39 x 46 cm), if desired.

DIRECTIONS

Mark the horizontal and vertical center of the fabric with basting thread, then cross-stitch the motif according to the chart, using two strands of floss over two threads of linen for each stitch.

Plum Vine Sampler

*"Who was it took such pains
To teach me very plain
With care to mark my name
my Aunt.
John Nichols
Hackleton
Aged 6, 1858"*

EMBROIDERY MEASUREMENTS

5-1/2 x 5-1/2 in. (14 x 14 cm)

MATERIALS

A piece of ecru linen 11-3/4 x 11-3/4 in. (30 x 30 cm) with 30 threads per inch (12 per cm); DMC or Anchor embroidery floss as indicated on the key to the chart plus very dark wine #221 or #897; frame (optional).

DIRECTIONS

Mark the horizontal and vertical center of the fabric with basting thread, then cross-stitch the motif according to the chart using two strands of floss over two threads of linen for each stitch.

Embroider the plums in outline stitch over completed cross-stitch using one strand of very dark wine floss #221 or #897.

KEY TO CHART

		DMC	Anchor
⋉	= medium wine	223	895
		= wine	224	893
✕	= blue black	336	150
||	= medium dark pine	501	878
∨	= gray green	522	860

		DMC	Anchor
∟	= light gray green	524	858
=	= dark sapphire	825	164
●	= sapphire	826	162
+	= dark gray green	926	850
−	= gray green	927	849

		DMC	Anchor
·	= light gray green	928	274
⌐	= blush	3354	74
⁒	= dark wine	3721	896

Christmas
Sampler

*"The smarting Whip-stitch,
Back-stitch and the Crosse-stitch,
All these are good and we must allow
And these are everywhere in practise now."*

—JOHN TAYLOR, "THE PRAISE OF THE NEEDLE," 1631

FINISHED MEASUREMENTS

15-1/2 x 24 in. (39.5 x 61.5 cm)

EMBROIDERY MEASUREMENTS

14-1/4 x 22-1/2 in. (36.5 x 58 cm)

MATERIALS

21-1/2 x 31-1/4 in. (55 x 80 cm) of white linen with 25 threads per inch (10 per cm); embroidery floss as indicated on the key to the chart; a matching frame (optional).

DIRECTIONS

Mark the horizontal and vertical center of the fabric with basting thread, then cross-stitch the motif according to the chart using two strands of floss over two threads of linen for each stitch. *Note: Work the light fawn #3774 or #376 cross-stitch in the hearth using one strand of floss.*

Continue the border around all sides to correspond to the right half.

Embroider in outline stitch over completed cross-stitch using two strands of floss:

- blue black #336 or #150 to outline the Christmas bells, the evergreen branches, the wreath bow, the large Christmas tree, the flame of the candle, the top and the front of the rocking horse's head, and the bows of the packages;
- medium pine #502 or #877 to outline the harness of the rocking horse;
- brick #356 or #5975 to outline the open hearth and the rocking horse;
- very dark fawn #632 or #936 to outline the Santa in the ornament;
- light carmine #815 or #43 for the large stitches of the Christmas stocking;
- and for all remaining outline stitches, medium dark coral #347 or #1025.

Design Note: You might want to embroider the small Christmas motifs separately on Christmas cards, clothing, placecards, or table linen or use them on tree decorations.

KEY TO CHART

		DMC	Anchor
• = white		white	1
◢ = blue black		336	150
⊠ = medium dark coral		347	1025
⌄ = brick		356	5975

CHRISTMAS SAMPLER

Symbol	Description	DMC	Anchor
⊡	= dark pine	500	879
◪	= medium dark pine	501	878
+	= medium pine	502	877
−	= light pine	503	875

Symbol	Description	DMC	Anchor
⊡	= very light pine	504	1042
◣	= very dark fawn	632	936
◪	= medium light copper	758	882
◪	= medium light coral	760	1022

Symbol	Description	DMC	Anchor
●	= light carmine	815	43
◪	= dark salmon	817	13
◳	= medium cocoa	3773	1008
▯	= light fawn	3774	376

Nautical Sampler

FROM A SAMPLER HONORING
GEORGE WASHINGTON'S INAUGURATION:

*"Pitch upon that course of life
which is the most excellent,
and habit will render it the
most delightful…
Mary Varick. 1789. New York."*

FINISHED MEASUREMENTS

17 x 21 in. (43.5 x 54 cm)

EMBROIDERY MEASUREMENTS

15-1/2 x 19-1/2 in. (40 x 50 cm)

MATERIALS

23-1/2 x 27-1/4 in. (60 x 70 cm) of double-thread canvas with 7-1/2 mesh
holes per inch (3 per cm); embroidery floss or DMC embroidery cotton
as indicated on the key to the chart; (optional) a frame, or a piece of
pressboard 17 x 21 in. (43.5 x 54 cm) and a piece of flannel 23-1/2 x
27-1/4 in. (60 x 70 cm).

DIRECTIONS

Mark the horizontal and vertical center of the fabric with basting thread
and cross-stitch the motif according to the chart. For both cross-stitches
and outline stitches, use one strand of embroidery cotton or six strands
of floss over one mesh hole for each stitch.

Replace the word "boudewign" in the lower left of the sampler with
the name or boat name of your choice, using letters from either of the
alphabets.

Embroider in outline stitch over completed cross-stitch, using the same
colors as the cross-stitches.

If you wish, frame your embroidery or cover the pressboard with the
flannel and stretch your sampler over it.

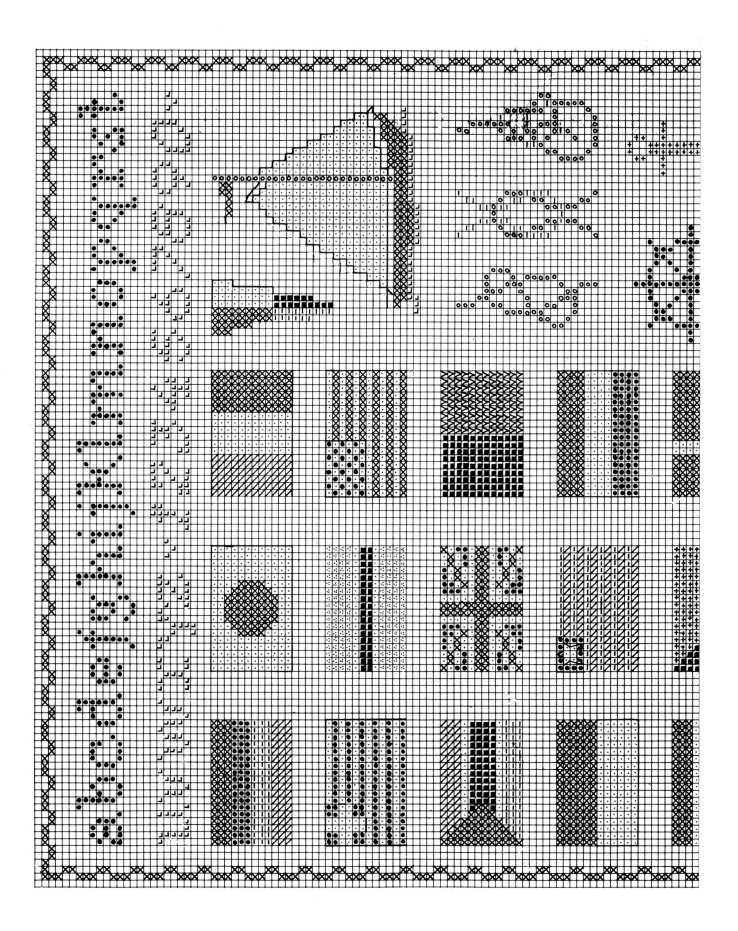

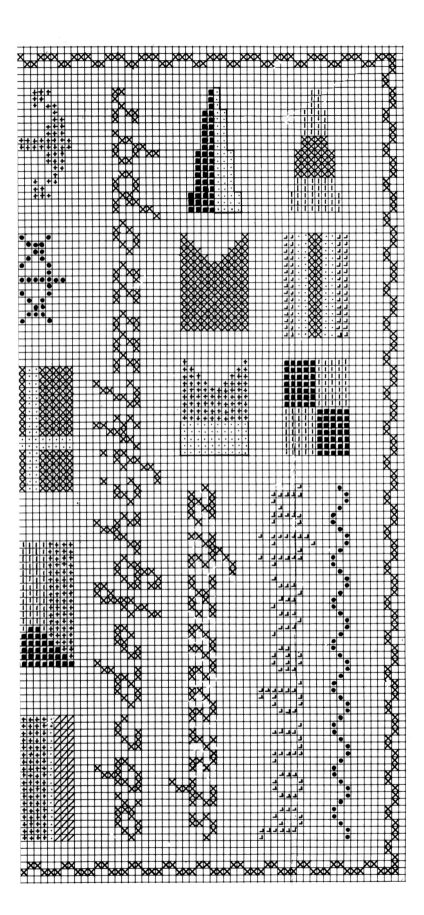

KEY TO CHART

	DMC Floss	Anchor Floss	DMC Cotton
• = white	white	1	white
■ = black	310	403	2310
○ = light toast	436	1045	2767
╎ = medium yellow	444	290	2444
⊠ = light red	666	46	2666
◺ = carmine	815	44	2815

	DMC Floss	Anchor Floss	DMC Cotton
● = dark navy	820	134	2820
∴ = light delft	828	975	2828
╱ = dark mint green	911	205	2911
╀ = dark peacock blue	995	410	2995
⌐ = peacock blue	996	433	2996

31

Flower Basket Samplers

"In the country life of America there are many moments when a woman can have recourse to nothing but her needle for employment."

—THOMAS JEFFERSON TO HIS DAUGHTER MARTHA, 1787

EMBROIDERY MEASUREMENTS

Large sampler: 17 x 20-3/4 in. (43.5 x 53 cm)
Small sampler: 14-1/2 x 16-1/4 in. (37 x 41.5 cm)

MATERIALS

For the large sampler, 25-1/4 x 33 in. (65 x 85 cm) and for the small sampler 21-1/2 x 23-1/2 in. (55 x 60 cm) of white linen with 30 threads per inch (12 per cm); embroidery floss as indicated on the key to the charts; matching frames, if desired.

DIRECTIONS

After marking the horizontal and vertical center of the fabric with basting thread, cross-stitch the motifs according to each chart, using two strands of floss over two threads of linen for each stitch.

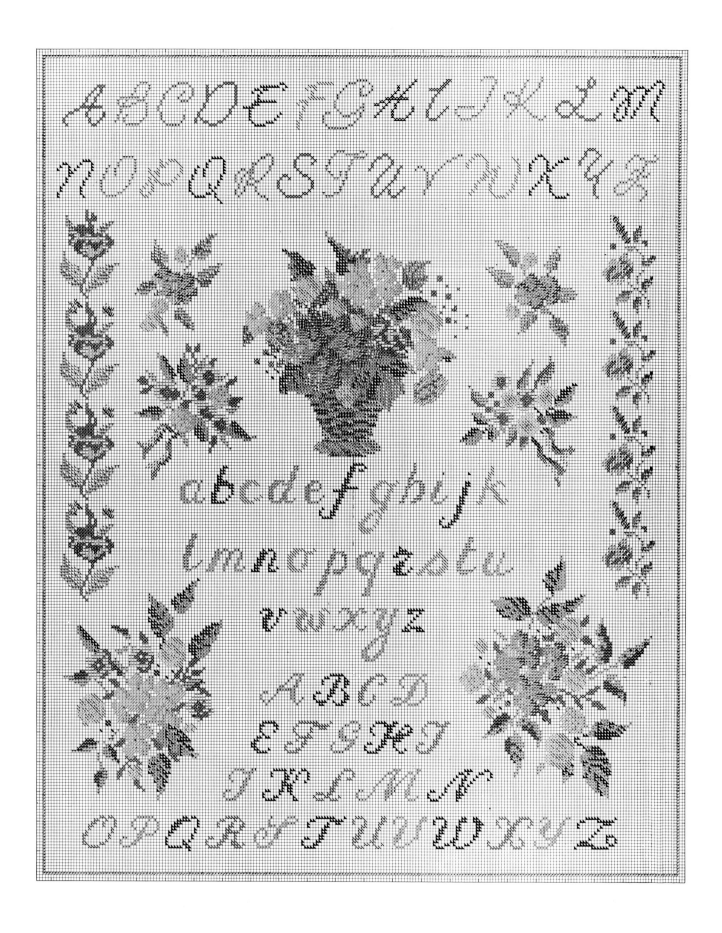

KEY TO CHARTS

Symbol	Color	DMC	Anchor
●	= medium wine	223	895
∨	= medium light wine	224	894
＼	= light wine	225	892
＼	= plum	316	969
✕	= medium jade	368	214
＼	= tan	437	362
⌐	= light moss green	472	842
✕	= light pine	503	875
／	= light jade	504	213
●	= gray green	522	860
Ｚ	= medium desert	612	832
Ｉ	= light harvest	613	956
⁊	= very light desert	644	831

Symbol	Color	DMC	Anchor
∴	= camel	676	891
•	= very light ecru	712	926
∷	= medium peach	744	301
∷	= light tan	738	361
⁒	= med. lt. terra cotta	758	337
−	= very lt. loden green	772	259
⌐	= pink	776	24
○	= wine	778	893
L	= copper	945	881
⌐	= medium light beige	950	4146
⌐	= light copper	951	880
◤	= medium moss green	3012	844
●	= moss green	3013	843

Symbol	Color	DMC	Anchor
◥	= med. light amethyst	3041	871
H	= amethyst	3042	870
∨	= light watermelon	3326	36
Ｎ	= very light avocado	3348	264
Ｔ	= lt. avocado (Anchor)	3348	265
⌐	= light loden green	3364	260
⁄	= light lilac	3609	95
∴	= very light coral	3713	968
＝	= light amethyst	3743	869
∙⁖	= light beige	3774	778
＋	= medium beige	3779	868

Memorial Sampler

"O may I seize the transient hour
Improve each moment as it flies
Lifes a short summer — man a flower
He dies — Alas — how soon he dies
Wrought by Clarinda Parker aged 13 years
August 3 Anno Domini 1824"

EMBROIDERY MEASUREMENTS

20-1/2 x 24-1/4 in. (52.5 x 62.5 cm)

MATERIALS

29-1/4 x 33 in. (75 x 85 cm) of ecru linen with 30 threads per inch (12 per cm); embroidery floss as indicated on the key to the chart; frame (optional).

DIRECTIONS

After marking the horizontal and vertical center of the fabric with basting thread, cross-stitch the sampler according to the chart using two strands of floss over two threads of fabric for each stitch.

Embroider the appropriate initials and dates in the motifs using the upper alphabet. Fill in the little areas in the peacock's tail with vertical satin stitches — the colors are indicated in each little area. For the peacock's feet, first work all the half-crosses in yellow one way, and then, working in the other direction, stitch the half-crosses over them in black to create complete cross-stitches.

Design Note: Samplers stitched in someone's memory were common in the eighteenth and nineteenth centuries. If you wish, use small beads to embroider your own initials in the center of the flower wreath, and a date of your own choosing in the lowest motif, using the upper alphabet.

KEY TO CHART

	DMC	Anchor			DMC	Anchor			DMC	Anchor
■ = black	310	403		= camel	676	891	∴ = very light beige	948	1011
◩ = medium dark beige	407	914	◿ = olive green	734	279	◺ = light khaki	3013	842
◣ = dark fog	451	233	= light sand	739	885	▶ = dark tawny	3021	905
∴ = chartreuse	471	255	◩ = medium saffron	834	874	= linen	3033	391
● = medium dark pine	501	878	◨ = dark fawn	840	379	◺ = medium light sand	3046	887
✕ = medium pine	502	877	◩ = medium fawn	841	378	◢ = med. lt. sand/black	3046/310	887/403
◤ = medium dark sand	610	936	o = medium ecru	842	388	S = medium copper	3064	883
⊠ = very dark fawn	632	393	◿ = dark terra cotta	918	341	◣ = avocado	3346	267
= dark linen	640	392	◖ = dark aquamarine	924	851	● = med. dk. loden green	3363	262
◿ = medium linen	642	392	∴ = med. lt. aquamarine	926	850			
· = very light desert	644	830	∴ = light aquamarine	927	849			

Circus Sampler

*"Dear mother I am young and cannot show
such work as I unto your goodness owe
Be pleased to smile on this my small endeavour
Ill strive to learn and be obedient ever....
Mary Ann Body
her work in y 9
year of her age 1789"*

FINISHED MEASUREMENTS

21-3/4 x 27-1/2 in. (56 x 71 cm)

EMBROIDERY MEASUREMENTS

19-1/2 x 25-1/4 in. (50 x 65 cm)

MATERIALS

27 x 33 in. (69.5 x 85 cm) of Aida cloth with 11 thread groups
per inch (4 to 4.5 per cm); embroidery floss as indicated on the
key to the chart; frame (optional).

DIRECTIONS

Mark the horizontal and vertical center of the fabric with basting
thread. Cross-stitch the motif according to the chart, using three
strands of floss over one thread group of fabric for each stitch.

Embroider in outline stitch over completed cross-stitch, using
two strands of floss:
- around the horses in gray #318 or #399;
- around the girl in the ring in medium melon #3340 or #329;
  around the lions in desert #611 or #898;
- and around all remaining figures with black #310 or #403.

Use black #310 or #403 to satin stitch the lions' noses and to
embroider all eyes in French knots.

KEY TO CHART

		DMC	Anchor
·	= white	white	1
■	= black	310	403
◪	= gray	318	399
∴	= medium nutmeg	422	373
●	= desert	611	898
∨	= light red	666	46
Z	= dark bottle green	701	227
∩	= light camel	729	890
│	= silver	762	234
+	= medium dark topaz	783	308
⊠	= light navy	797	132
○	= medium cobalt	809	130
⟍	= medium rose	893	41
╱	= dark pink	894	26
∷	= light copper	951	880
◺	= medium jonquil	973	297
∨	= peacock blue	996	433
⁒	= medium melon	3340	329

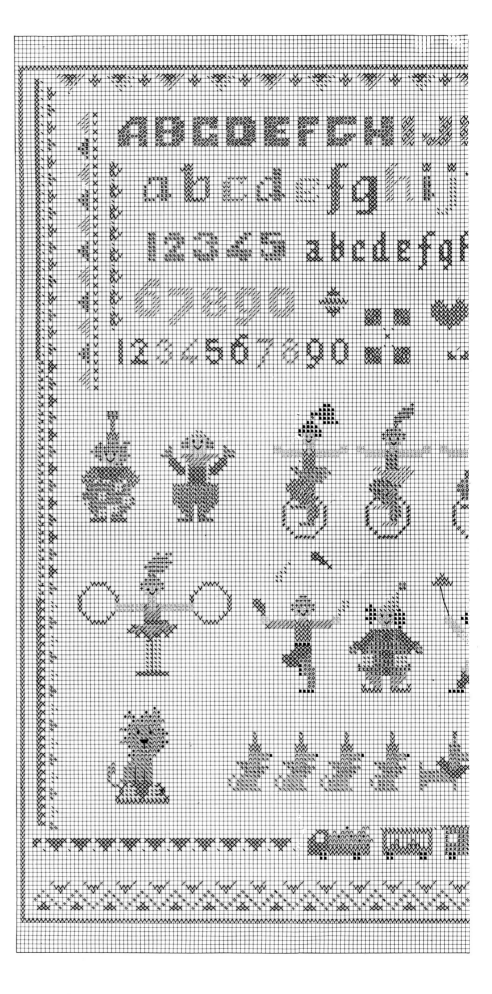

Blue Birth Sampler

FROM ELEVEN-YEAR-OLD RACHEL ELLICOTT'S 1827 SAMPLER:

*"Almighty power whose tender care did infancy protect,
Let riper years thy favour share and every step direct
Rachel Ellicott
1827"*

FINISHED MEASUREMENTS

14-3/4 x 19 in. (38 x 48.5 cm)

EMBROIDERY MEASUREMENTS

11-3/4 x 15-3/4 in. (30 x 40.5 cm)

MATERIALS

19 x 19 in. (49 x 49 cm) of white linen with 25 threads per inch (10 per cm); two skeins of light blue embroidery floss (DMC #3753 or Anchor #1031); white embroidery cotton #20 and #25; a matching frame, if desired.

DIRECTIONS

Use basting thread to mark the horizontal and vertical center of the fabric. Embroider the motif according to the chart, using two strands of floss for each stitch. Work each cross-stitch over two threads of linen and each star stitch over four threads.

In the open area, embroider the name and birth date. Embroider the name twenty threads above the date. (The European-style date here lists the month first.)

For the openwork border, use embroidery cotton #25 to work a ladder hemstitch (see the Appendix), gathering four threads for each stitch. Work a small openwork row between the name and cursive letters and large openwork above and below the embroidery work, as shown in the photo, over eight threads.

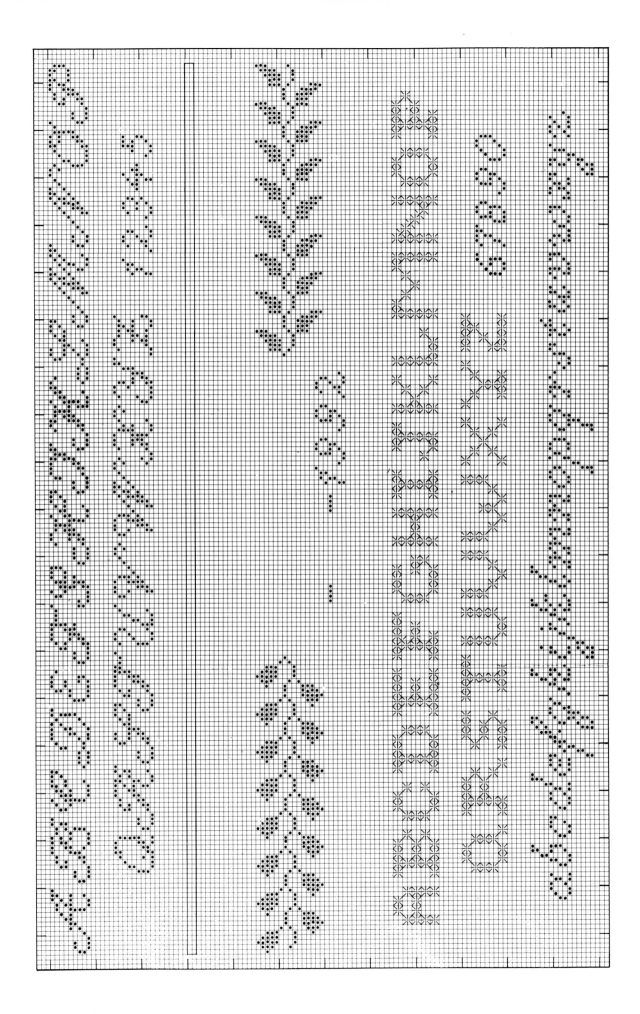

Paper Doll Samplers

FROM TWELVE-YEAR-OLD MARY RICHARDSON'S 1783 SAMPLER:

*"This Needle Work Of Mine Can Tell When A
Child Is Learned Well By My Parants I Was
Tought Not To Spend My Time For Nought"*

FINISHED MEASUREMENTS

16-1/4 x 16-1/4 in. (41.5 x 41.5 cm) each

EMBROIDERY MEASUREMENTS

11-1/4 x 11-1/4 in. (29 x 29 cm) each

MATERIALS

For each sampler, 19-1/2 x 19-1/2 in. (50 x 50 cm) of linen with 25 threads per inch (10 per cm); embroidery floss as indicated on the key to the chart plus dark brown #838 or #380 for the boy only; a wooden frame (optional).

DIRECTIONS

For one sampler, after marking the horizontal and vertical center of the fabric with basting thread, cross-stitch the motif according to the chart, using two strands of floss over two threads of linen for each stitch.

When stitching the border, embroider the name in the center top border and a birth date or other iden-

tifier in the center bottom border, if you wish. (See the section "Starting Out" for centering tips.) Either design your own letters and numbers or adapt those from an alphabet in another sampler in the book. (The European-style date here lists the month first.)

Embroider in outline stitch over completed cross-stitch using two strands of floss over two threads of linen.

For the girl:
- the mouth and the hat in medium dark salmon #350 or #11;
- the body and face in light salmon #353 or #6;
- and the white tabs of the clothes in ocean blue #793 or #176.

For the boy:
- the mouth in dark salmon #817 or #13;
- the body and face in light salmon #353 or #6;
- the hats and the white tabs of the clothes in navy #796 or #133;
- and the bear in dark brown #838 or #380.

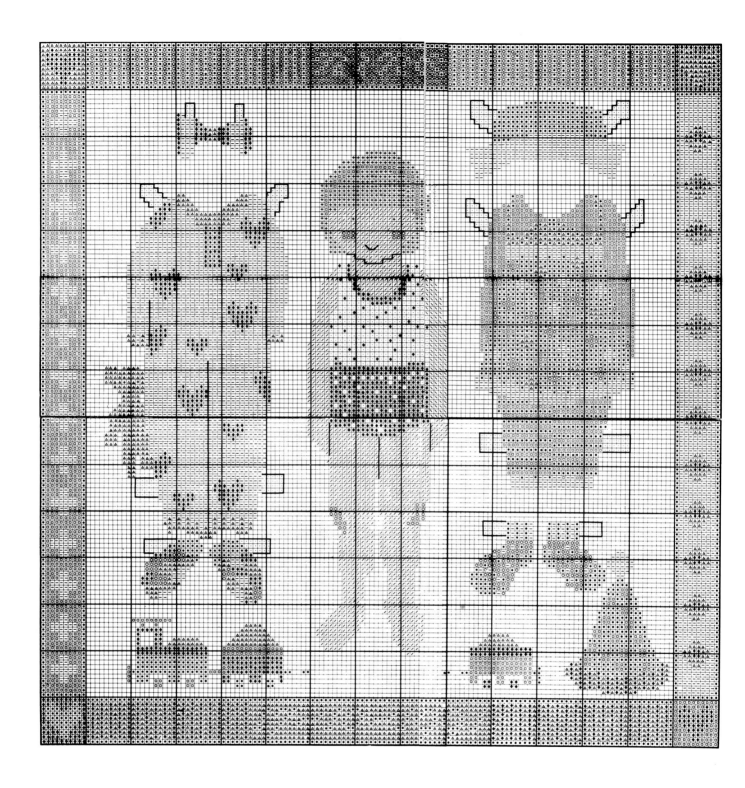

KEY TO CHART

GIRL

	DMC	Anchor			DMC	Anchor
⬚ = white	white	1		△ = light topaz	725	305
◆ = medium dark salmon	350	11		● = ocean blue	793	176
⊙ = light salmon	353	6		╱ = very light beige	948	1011
⊞ = dark mocha	433	357		▭ = light watermelon	3326	36
▢ = medium light teal	598	167				

KEY TO CHART

		DMC	Anchor				DMC	Anchor
•	= white	white	1	△	= light topaz		725	305
○	= light salmon	353	6	●	= navy		796	133
+	= dark mocha	433	357	◆	= dark salmon		817	13
□	= medium light teal	598	167	╱	= very light beige		948	1011
─	= dark bottle green	701	227					

Bows Birth Sampler

"Honor thy mother
For her arms
Secur'd thee from
A thousand harms.
Charlotte Frobisher,
aged 9
1805."

EMBROIDERY MEASUREMENTS

20 x 22-1/4 in. (51 x 57 cm)

MATERIALS

29-1/4 x 31-1/4 in. (75 x 80 cm) of Hardanger cloth with 11 threads per inch (4.5 per cm); embroidery floss as indicated on the key to the chart; frame (optional).

DIRECTIONS

After marking the horizontal and vertical center of the fabric with basting thread, cross-stitch the motif according to the chart using three strands of floss over one thread of fabric for each stitch. Use the alphabet and numbers in the sampler to substitute the appropriate name and date. (The European-style date on the pictured sampler lists the month first.)

KEY TO CHART

		DMC	Anchor
·	= white	white	1
■	= black	310	403
⊠	= jade	320	215
●	= medium watermelon	335	38
◆	= light topaz	725	305
◇	= light jonquil	727	293
○	= pink	776	24
×	= light sapphire	813	161
✗	= very dark delft	825	979
⊡	= sapphire	826	162
□	= medium glacier blue	827	159
△	= medium blossom pink	899	52
▲	= forest green	912	209
△	= light lime	966	240
◉	= dark tangerine	971	316
⊙	= light watermelon	3326	36

51

Nursery Sampler

FROM A SALEM, MASSACHUSETTS, SAMPLER,
BY NABY DANE, AGE TWELVE:

"Naby Dane Her Sampler
Wrought June The 27 1789
Born July The 19 1777
Next Unto God
Dear Parents I Address MySelf To you
In Humble Thankfulness
For All your Care
And Charge On me"

FINISHED MEASUREMENTS

20-1/2 x 27 in. (52.5 x 69.5 cm)

EMBROIDERY MEASUREMENTS

15-1/4 x 21-1/2 in. (39 x 55 cm)

MATERIALS

25-1/4 x 31-1/4 in. (65 x 80 cm) of Hardanger fabric with 22-1/2 threads per inch (9 per cm); embroidery floss as indicated on the key to the chart; if desired, a frame 20-1/2 x 27 in. (52.5 x 69.5 cm).

DIRECTIONS

Mark the horizontal and vertical center of the fabric with basting thread. Cross-stitch the motif according to the chart, using three strands of floss over two threads of fabric for each stitch.

Insert the desired name in the space at the bottom center of the chart, using letters from the upper alphabet, with the birth date centered above it, using whichever numbers you choose (see the section "Starting Out" for spacing tips). (The birth date in the picture lists the month first, European style.)

KEY TO CHART

		DMC	Anchor
■	= black	310	403
●	= brick	356	5975
✕	= med. dark pine	501	878
○	= med. light copper	758	882
◇	= med. saffron	834	874
□	= denim blue	932	920

Mama
and
Papa Bear
Samplers

FROM A 1769 SAMPLER:

*"When in Love I do commence
May it be with a man of sense
Brisk and arey may he be
Free from a spirit of jealousy."*

EMBROIDERY MEASUREMENTS

11 x 11 in. (28 x 28 cm)

MATERIALS

For each portrait, 15-1/2 x 15-1/2 in. (40 x 40 cm) of counted cross-stitch fabric with 25 threads per inch (10 per cm); embroidery floss as indicated on the key to the charts; frames, if desired.

DIRECTIONS

After marking the vertical and horizontal center of the fabric with basting thread, cross-stitch the motif according to the charts, using four strands of floss over four threads of fabric.

Embroider in outline stitch over completed cross-stitch, following the key for outline stitches and the chart.

KEY TO CHARTS

		DMC	Anchor
∴	= ecru	ecru	387
⊠	= black	310	403
⊞	= red	321	9046
⊡	= medium watermelon	335	38
●	= dark mocha	433	357
⬦	= brown	434	370
◺	= chartreuse	470	256
—	= sand	677	886
⊠	= light topaz	725	305
○	= dark topaz	781	309
·	= topaz	783	307
▼	= ocean blue	793	176
◹	= light ocean blue	794	175
◆	= dark coffee	898	360
‖	= medium sand	3045	888
△	= light denim	3752	343

Outline Stitches

		DMC	Anchor
∿	= black	310	403
⌣⌣	= red	321	9046
- - - -	= dark mocha	433	357
——	= med. ocean blue	792	177
— —	= ocean blue	793	176
•—•—•	= dark fawn	840	379

Carnival Sampler

FROM AN 1800 SAMPLER BY PATTY POLK, AGE TEN, KENT, MARYLAND:

*"Patty Polk did this
and she hated every stitch
she did in it.
She loves to read
much more."*

EMBROIDERY MEASUREMENTS

46-1/2 x 26 in. (119 x 67 cm)

MATERIALS

54-1/2 x 35 in. (140 x 90 cm) of cream-colored cotton with 17.5 threads per inch (7 per cm.); embroidery floss as indicated on the key to the chart; black DMC pearl cotton #8 or the equivalent; a frame or a piece of chipboard 46-1/2 x 26 in. (119 x 67 cm), if desired.

DIRECTIONS

Mark the horizontal and vertical center of the fabric with basting thread, then cross-stitch the carnival motifs according to the chart, using four strands of floss over two threads of fabric for each stitch.

Outline stitch over completed cross-stitch, using three strands of floss:

- dark red orange #606 or #335 for the mouths;
- for the whirler on the right, dark red orange #606 or #335 for the middle section and dark jonquil #972 or #298 in the scallops around the roof;
- navy #796 or #133 for the pigtailed girl at the lower right, the boy with the yo-yo, the girl with the balloon, and the boy with the dark red orange cap;
- and the remaining outline stitches in black #310 or #403.

For the lines under the children, use black #310 or #403, navy #796 or #133, or light charcoal #317 or #400.

Make long straight stitches in black pearl cotton #8 for the lines of the whirlers, the balloons, and the yo-yo.

Embroider the border in satin stitch with six strands of floss. (Refer to the border chart in the upper right

corner of the large chart.) For one square on the chart, make two small satin stitches over two fabric threads. Then use one strand of the same color to make a row of running stitches below the satin stitches. Beginning at the lower right corner of the border, embroider sixty-seven blue triangles along the bottom border. After working the lower left corner,

embroider thirty-six blue triangles along the left side border. Repeat for the top and right side.

If you wish, frame the finished needlework or stretch it over the chipboard.

Design Note:
Each of the figures can also be made as an individual picture for small samplers, cards, towels, clothing, soft blocks, and other children's items.

KEY TO CHART

		DMC	Anchor			DMC	Anchor			DMC	Anchor
•	= white	white	1	�);	= light charcoal	317	400	⊠	= dark red orange	606	335
▼	= dark bark	300	352	▽	= gray	318	399	∷	= light desert	613	831
		= yellow	307	289	◟	= light gray	415	398	O	= emerald	702	239
■	= black	310	403	∨	= light rosebud pink	604	55	—	= medium light copper	758	882

		DMC	Anchor			DMC	Anchor			DMC	Anchor
•⁚	= silver	762	234	N	= dark sapphire	825	164	☐	= peacock blue	996	433
●	= navy	796	133	∴	= copper	945	881	L	= medium sand	3045	888
◣	= medium blue	798	142	Z	= dark tangerine	970	316				
⁘	= light cobalt	809	130	╱	= dark jonquil	972	298				

Butterfly Birth Sampler

FROM A NINETEENTH-CENTURY SAMPLER
STITCHED IN PETERBOROUGH, NEW HAMPSHIRE:

"Youth the spring time of our years
Short the rapid scene appears
let's improve the fleeting hours
Virtue's noblest fruits be ours
Wrought by Sally Abbot aged 11 years.
June 6th 1818"

FINISHED MEASUREMENTS

17-1/2 x 17-1/2 in. (45 x 45 cm)

MATERIALS

White Hardanger cloth 22 x 22 in. (56.5 x 56.5 cm) with 23 double threads per inch (9 per cm); embroidery floss as indicated on the key to the chart; frame, if desired.

DIRECTIONS

After marking the horizontal and vertical center of the fabric with basting thread, cross-stitch the motif according to the chart, using three strands of floss over two double threads of fabric for each stitch.

Outline stitch over completed cross-stitch, using three strands of floss:

- very dark bark #400 or #351 around the cat;
- red orange #606 or #334 around the windows of the house;
- and black #310 or #403 for the remaining figures.

Work satin stitches for the animals' mouths (see the photo) using three strands of black #310 or #403. Stem stitch the whiskers of the rabbits and cat with two strands of black #310 or #403, and the rooster's feet with three strands of light emerald #700 or #228.

Use the alphabet and numbers in the sampler to substitute the appropriate name and date. (The European-style date on the pictured sampler lists the month first.)

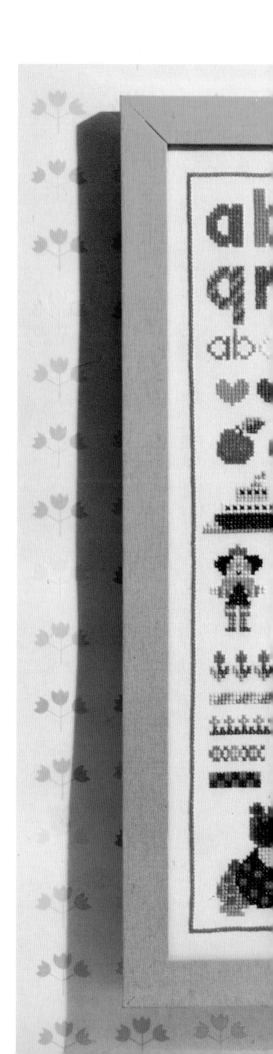

d e f g h i j k l m n o p
t u v w x y z 1 2 3 4 5 6 7 8 9
1 2 3 4 5 6 7 8 9 0 · 0
f g h i j k l m n o p q r s t u v w x y z

peter

13·10·1981

KEY TO CHART

		DMC	Anchor
·	= white	white	1
◥	= black	310	403
◿	= gray	318	399
◖	= dark red	321	47
◑	= very dark bark	400	351
L	= medium yellow	444	290
◤	= violet	552	99
●	= medium magenta	603	62
◪	= red orange	606	334
◡	= light desert	613	831
N	= light emerald	700	228
∴	= light jonquil	727	293
◺	= dark orange	741	304
◣	= navy	796	133
◞	= medium glacier blue	827	159
▼	= dark coffee	898	360
S	= parrot green	905	257
O	= dark chartreuse	907	255
∵	= copper	945	881
◿	= dark melon	947	330
⊠	= peacock blue	996	433
◹	= medium sand	3045	888

Schoolroom Sampler

"While I with care my work pursue
And to my book my mind apply
Ill keep my teachrs love in view
And guard my way with watch
ful eye…
Wrought by Rebecca J Wild
Charlestown Jan 1 1831
Aged 10 years"

FINISHED MEASUREMENTS

18-3/4 x 28 in. (48 x 72)

EMBROIDERY MEASUREMENTS

17-1/2 x 27 in. (45 x 69 cm)

MATERIALS

25-1/4 x 35 in. (65 x 90 cm) of white double-thread canvas with 7-1/2 mesh holes per inch (3 per cm); DMC embroidery cotton (or its equivalent) as indicated on the key to the chart plus ecru and pale blue #2828; (optional) frame or pressboard 17-1/2 x 27 in. (45 x 69 cm).

DIRECTIONS

Mark the horizontal and vertical center of the canvas with basting thread. Using one strand of embroidery cotton over one mesh hole for each stitch, cross-stitch the motif according to the chart.

Use other stitches for the following figures (see the Appendix):

- for the baseboard, use vertical satin stitches;
- for the books, use horizontal satin stitches;
- for the windowsills, use horizontal and vertical satin stitches;
- for the curtain rod, use vertical satin stitches over a long straight stitch;
- for the little red flowers in the plant, make French knots;
- for the drapes, use half cross-stitches over a long straight stitch;

- for the blackboard, use half cross-stitches and then run one strand in diagonal lines beneath them;
- for the sky, use running stitches in pale blue #2828 cotton: run one strand through the large mesh holes (up one, down one) and another strand through the narrow mesh holes to create a woven effect (refer to the photo);
- for the floor, use ecru running stitches for fourteen rows below the bottom line of cross-stitches; run two strands through the large mesh holes and

one strand through the narrow mesh holes
- for the teacher's necklace, use one dark blue strand in which you make knots to simulate beads.

Outline stitch over completed cross-stitch with one strand of cotton:
- turquoise #2996 around the blue-green bag;
- dark blue #2825 around the turquoise bag;
- blue #2827 in and around the dark blue bags;
- dark blue #2825 for the numbers on the clock;
- beige #2613 for the line along the windowsills and the bear's ear;
- dark brown #2839 for the teacher's eyebrows, around the desks and bookshelves, and around the animals (except the goat and the duck's head);
- and brown #2609 for all other outline stitches.

If you wish, frame the embroidery or stretch it around the pressboard.

KEY TO CHART

		DMC Cotton			DMC Cotton			DMC Cotton
•	= white	white	◢	= green	2561	∷	= pink	2758
●	= black	2310	△	= blue green	2595	▼	= dark blue	2825
⦗⦘	= gray	2318	⊠	= brown	2609	L	= blue	2827
+	= red	2349			= beige	2613	▽	= dark brown	2839
○	= light green	2471	◺	= yellow	2727	◿	= turquoise	2996

69

Pastel Birth Sampler

FROM A 1681 SAMPLER BY MARGARET LUCUS:

"My father hitherto hath done his best to make me a workewoman above the rest. Margreet Lucuh 1681 bezng ten year old come July the first."

FINISHED MEASUREMENTS

15-1/2 x 18-3/4 in. (40 x 48 cm)

EMBROIDERY MEASUREMENTS

10-1/2 x 13-3/4 in. (27 x 35.5 cm)

Note: The motifs can be extended to accommodate a longer name.

MATERIALS

Hardanger cloth 19-1/2 x 23-1/2 in. (50 x 60 cm) with 23 thread groups per inch (9 per cm); embroidery floss as indicated on the key to the chart; frame (optional).

DIRECTIONS

Cross-stitch the motif according to the chart using three strands of floss over two fabric threads for each stitch. Begin embroidering in the upper right-hand corner 2-1/2 in. (6.5 cm) from the edge of the fabric. Repeat motif 1 four times. Embroider the rest of the sampler one set of motifs at a time, so that stitching for each set ends at the same place on the left side of the sampler (see photo).

To embroider the name and date, mark the center by stitching a line of basting down the middle of your piece, using the top motif as a guide. Center the name and date where "1993" appears on the chart, according to the instructions in the section "Starting Out." (You can choose letters from an alphabet on one of the other samplers in the book or design your own.) Embroider the name and date first, then embroider the motif on each side. (The pictured sampler lists the month first, European style.)

When you have completed all eight sets of motifs, embroider the border according to the chart.

KEY TO CHART

		DMC	Anchor
☐	= medium jade	368	214
•	= camel	676	891
⊠	= light coral	761	1021
●	= ocean blue	793	176
○	= light ocean blue	794	175
✗	= dark blush	3733	75

Home Sweet Home Sampler

"Tell me ye knowing and discerning few
Where I may find a Friend both firm and true
Who dares stand by me when in deep distress
And then his Love and Friendship dost express
Mary Ann Richards her Work
June The First 1800"

FINISHED MEASUREMENTS

13 x 16-1/2 in. (33.5 x 42 cm)

EMBROIDERY MEASUREMENTS

11-3/4 x 14-3/4 in. (30 x 38 cm)

MATERIALS

21-1/2 x 23-1/2 in. (55 x 60 cm) of linen with 25 threads per inch (10 per cm); DMC or Anchor embroidery floss as indicated in the key to the chart plus juniper #367 or #217, raspberry #3687 or #68, and delft #334 or #977; frame, if desired.

DIRECTIONS

After marking the horizontal and vertical center of the fabric with basting thread, cross-stitch the sampler using two strands of floss over two threads of linen for each stitch.

Embroider in outline stitch over completed cross-stitch using one strand of floss:

* around the plum flowers with raspberry #3687 or #68;
* in and around the light delft flowers and the light seafoam centers of the blooming roses in delft #334 or #977;
* along the roof, the lower edge of the house, the window frames, the bench, the flower pots, the light topaz flowers, and in and around the basket with pine #503 or #876.

Embroider all remaining outline stitches in juniper #367 or #217.

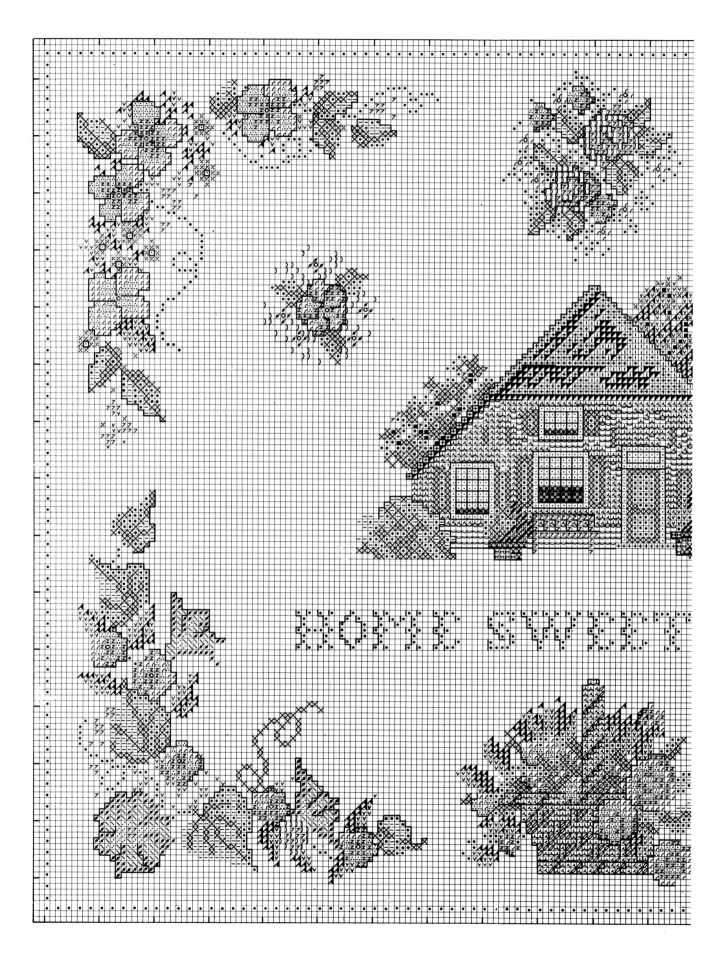

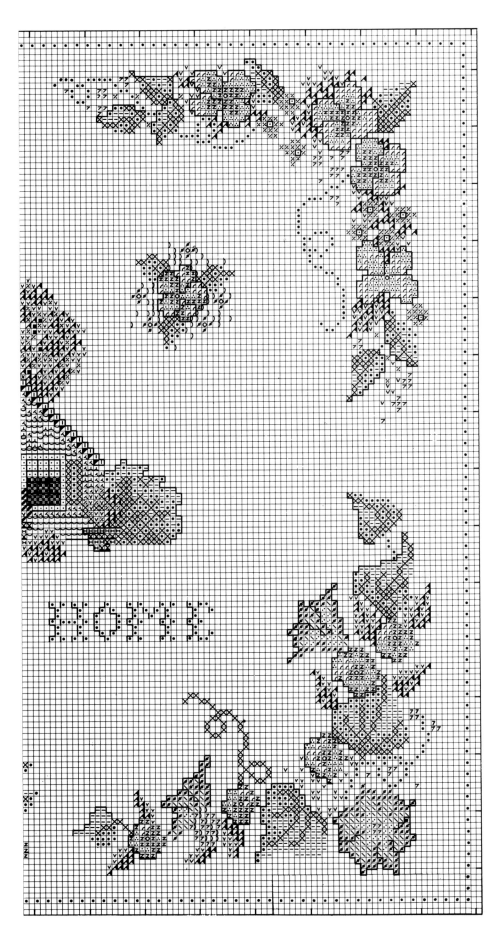

KEY TO CHART

		DMC	Anchor
•	= white	white	1
	= off-white	white	2
	= medium wine	223	895
	= light wine	225	892
Z	= plum	316	969
	= jade	320	216
●	= medium jade	368	214
H	= light cinnamon	402	347
	= medium nutmeg	422	373
7	= tan	437	362
	= medium pine	502	877
◀	= pine	503	876
v	= light pine	504	875
	= pewter	646	8581
	= sand	677	886
O	= light topaz	725	305
	= light sand	739	885
	= peach	745	300
—	= light loden green	772	259
∴	= light plum	778	968
		= light linen	822	390
\	= light delft	828	975
◢	= terra cotta	921	338
•	= denim blue	932	920
∴	= light seafoam	3072	847
+	= light tawny	3782	899
■	= dark linen	3790	393
	= charcoal	3799	236

75

Caribbean Sampler

"Mary Bosworth, lately from London, takes this method to inform the public, that she has opened a school...wherein she teaches young masters and misses to read...learns young ladies plain work, samplairs, Dresden flowering on cat gut."

— THE *NEW YORK MERCURY*, 20 MAY 1765

EMBROIDERY MEASUREMENTS

37 x 37 in. (95 x 95 cm)

MATERIALS

44 x 44 in. (113 x 113 cm) of ecru linen with 13 threads per inch (5 per cm); Anchor embroidery wool (or its equivalent) as indicated on the key to the chart; frame, if desired.

DIRECTIONS

Mark the horizontal and vertical center of the fabric with basting thread, then embroider the motifs within the borders in cross-stitch, using one strand of wool over two threads of fabric for each stitch.

Next, embroider the lines between the squares in Rumanian stitch, using one strand of wool (see the Appendix). Stitches should be one thread high and ten threads wide.

Embroider the two red outlines in flannel stitch (see the Appendix) using one strand of wool, with stitches eight threads high and four threads wide. Work the corners as shown in the photo.

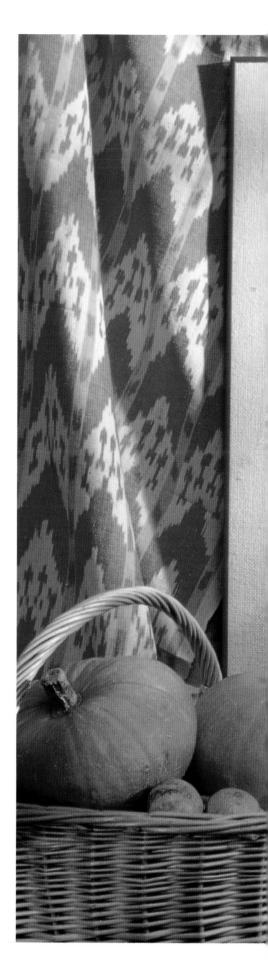

KEY TO CHART

		Anchor Yarn
◤	= rose	63
▼	= purple	107
◩	= blue	133
∴	= light blue	159
◣	= dark green	229
⊠	= green	239
∨	= olive green	279
—	= yellow	295
○	= orange	332
•	= white	402
■	= black	403
◠	= turquoise	567
∣	= pink	642
∨	= brown	650
⹀	= light brown	742
●	= red	748

Pastry Sampler

FROM AN 1820 SAMPLER BY
ELEANOR MALONE OF MASSACHUSETTS:

*"O may I with myself agree
And never covet what i see
content me with an humble shade
My passions tam'd my wishes laid
Wrought by
Eleanor Caroline Malone aged 8 years"*

FINISHED MEASUREMENTS

20-1/4 x 23-1/2 in. (52 x 60 cm)

EMBROIDERY MEASUREMENTS

17 x 19-1/2 in. (43.5 x 50 cm)

MATERIALS

28 x 31-1/4 in. (72 x 80 cm) of ecru linen with 25 threads per inch (10 per cm); DMC or Anchor embroidery floss as indicated on the key to the chart plus dark charcoal #535 or #400, dark turquoise #991 or #189, medium grape #3746 or #1030, and charcoal #3799 or #236; for the Hardanger border, Anchor white embroidery cotton #16 and #20 (or the equivalent); a frame, if desired.

DIRECTIONS

Mark the horizontal and vertical center of the fabric with basting thread. Using two strands of floss over two fabric threads for each stitch, cross-stitch the motif according to the chart.

Embroider in outline stitch over completed cross-stitch with one strand of floss:

- the names of the pastries with charcoal #3799 or #236;
- in and around the medium light pewter cake stands and the two chocolate cakes with dark charcoal #535 or #400;
- in and around the rest of the cakes with very dark fawn #632 or #936;
- in and around the upper right cake stand, the little dollops on the cakes, and the cake with the light maroon bow with very dark fawn #632 or #936 and with light toast #436 or #1045, as you prefer;
- in and around the remaining gold-colored stands with light toast #436 or #1045;
- in and around the light green decorations with dark turquoise #991 or #189;
- around the grape bow with medium grape #3746 or #1030;
- around the blossom pink bows, flowers, and decorations with medium watermelon #335 or #38;
- and around the light maroon bow with blossom pink #326 or #59.

Marquise
au chocolat blanc

Croque
en bouche

Charlotte
aux framboises

Charlotte
au citron

Vacherin
poire-marron

Charlotte
aux fraises

Charlotte
au chocolat

Charlotte
à la Russe

Double Diabolo
au chocolat

La Princesse
au meringue

Gâteau

81

KEY TO CHART

Symbol		DMC	Anchor	Symbol		DMC	Anchor	Symbol		DMC	Anchor
·	= white	white	1		= light pewter	648	900		= light maroon	961	76
●	= blossom pink	326	59		= sand	677	886	○	= light rust	977	1002
⊘	= medium watermelon	335	38	·.	= very light ecru	712	926	◗	= light green	988	243
◖	= grape	340	118	⊠	= light apricot	722	323		= linen	3033	391
+	= light grape	341	117		= light sand	739	885		= light seafoam	3072	847
Ζ	= medium jade	368	214	∟	= peach	745	300	＞	= very light avocado	3348	264
⊤	= light cinnamon	402	347	·.	= light peach	746	275	■	= very dark magenta	3350	65
Ħ	= medium dark beige	407	914		= very lt. loden green	772	259		= blush	3354	74
⟋	= medium nutmeg	422	373	⊠	= medium blossom pink	899	52	∷	= very light coral	3713	1020
⋀	= light toast	436	1045	·	= dark rust	922	1003	⋁	= medium pink	3716	25
=	= tan	437	362	n	= medium light beige	950	4146	∷	= light blueberry	3747	120
●	= very dark fawn	632	936		= light copper	951	880	⊠	= dark cocoa	3772	1007
⟋	= medium light pewter	647	1040	⟍	= blossom pink	957	50	⟋	= medium cocoa	3773	1008

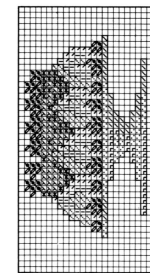

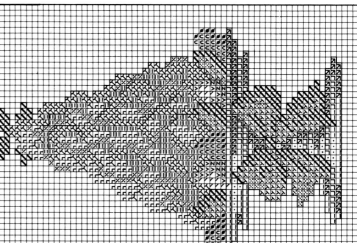

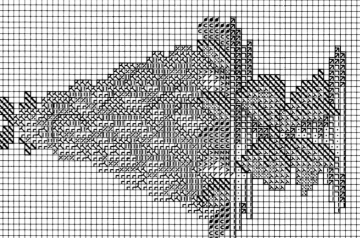

CHART 1

82

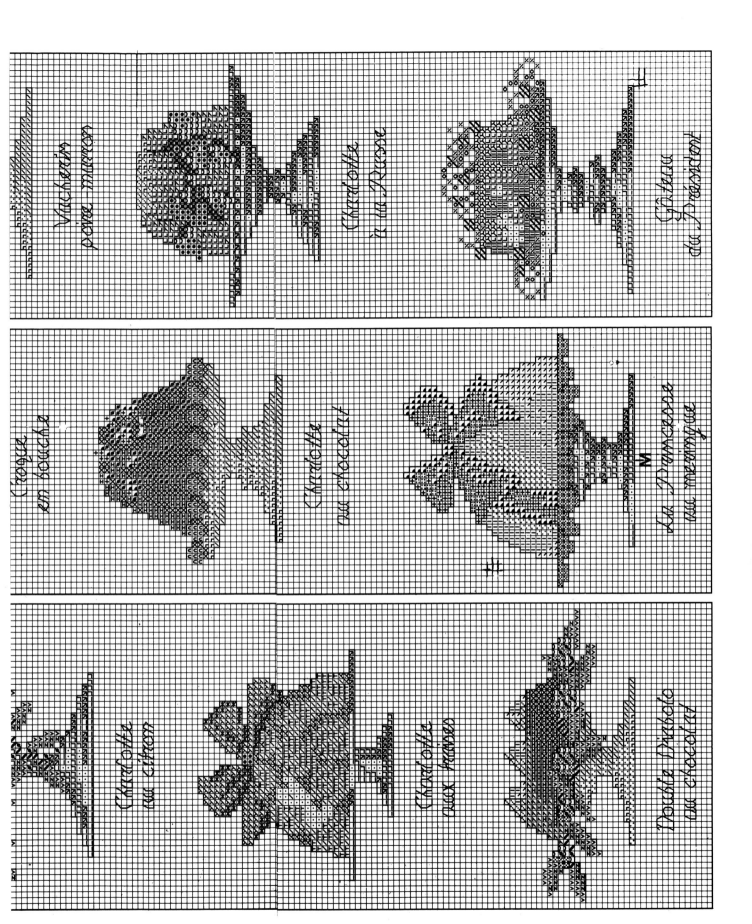

83

CHART 2

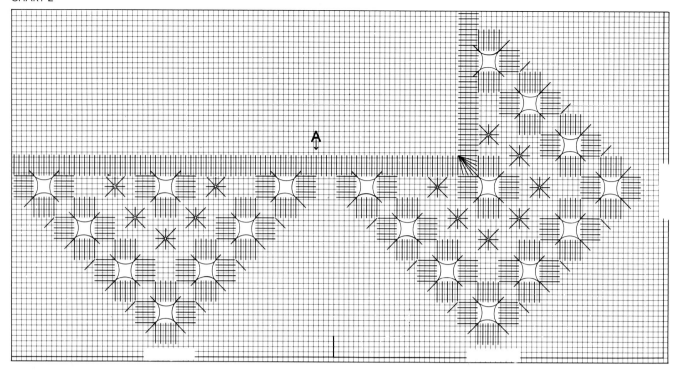

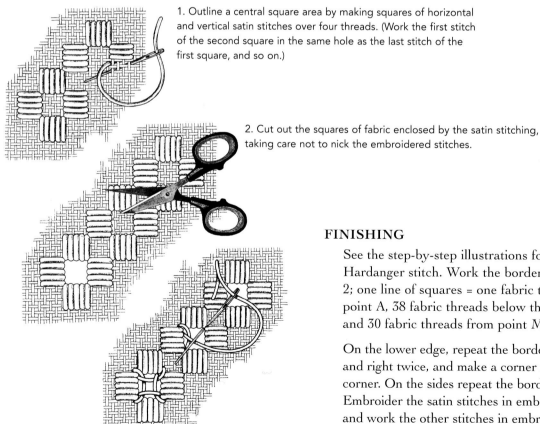

1. Outline a central square area by making squares of horizontal and vertical satin stitches over four threads. (Work the first stitch of the second square in the same hole as the last stitch of the first square, and so on.)

2. Cut out the squares of fabric enclosed by the satin stitching, taking care not to nick the embroidered stitches.

3. Refer to chart 2: decorate the open squares with a filling stitch that runs from corner to corner or with a star stitch.

FINISHING

See the step-by-step illustrations for working the Hardanger stitch. Work the border according to chart 2; one line of squares = one fabric thread. Begin at point A, 38 fabric threads below the center cake stand and 30 fabric threads from point M on chart 1.

On the lower edge, repeat the border motif to the left and right twice, and make a corner motif at each corner. On the sides repeat the border motif six times. Embroider the satin stitches in embroidery cotton #16, and work the other stitches in embroidery cotton #20. Follow the three-step directions for the border, working the satin stitches first, then cutting along the stitching to cut away the inside squares (white squares on chart 2). In the open squares, make filling stitches or star stitches, according to chart 2.

Home Celebration Sampler

FROM AN 1808 MARRIAGE SAMPLER BY MARY LEE:

"But happy they the happiest of their kind!
Whom gentler stars unite, and in one fate
Their hearts, their fortunes,
and their beings blend."

FINISHED MEASUREMENTS

26 x 27-1/4 in. (67 x 70 cm)

EMBROIDERY MEASUREMENTS

21 x 22-1/4 in. (54 x 57 cm)

MATERIALS

36 x 36 in. (92.5 x 92.5 cm) of white linen with 25 threads per inch (10 per cm); embroidery floss as indicated on the key to the chart; frame, if desired.

DIRECTIONS

Mark the horizontal and vertical center of the fabric with basting thread, then cross-stitch the motif according to the chart. Use two strands of floss over two fabric threads for each cross-stitch.

In the open areas, you may choose to embroider your own initials or those of the persons you wish to celebrate. Choose from the letters of the alphabet at the top of the sampler (change the size to suit your needs; see the section "Starting Out"). If you wish, embroider a date below the upper window of the house, as shown in the photo.

Embroider in outline stitch over completed cross-stitch, using two strands of floss:

- dark mint green #911 or #205 around the Christmas trees;
- orange #742 or #303 in and around the light orange flowers;
- medium blossom pink #899 or #52 in and around the pink and the pink-and-white flowers;
- medium spring green #703 or #238 around the white flowers in the border;

Design Note: This sampler makes a special gift for a new home or to celebrate a marriage or partnership or a new family member. The corner motifs reflect the seasons of the year.

- light apricot #722 or #323 around the light orange butterfly and around the light orange flowers beneath it;
- light rust #977 or #363 for the lines that emphasize the ears of wheat;
- gray #318 or #399 around the white flowers near the wheat;
- gray #318 or #399 or medium light amethyst #3041 or #871 for the butterflies' antennas;
- and black #310 or #403 in and around the berries and apples, around the sapphire butterflies, and in the centers of the light orange or light orange-and-white flowers.

KEY TO CHART

	DMC	Anchor
= white	white	1
= wine	224	893
= black	310	403
= gray	318	399
= light grape	341	117
= medium dark salmon	350	11
C = salmon	352	9
= very light lime	369	1043
= very dark topaz	434	310
= tan	437	362
= light chartreuse	472	253
= light pewter	648	900

	DMC	Anchor
= camel	676	891
= medium spring green	703	238
= light parrot green	704	256
= light apricot	722	323
= light topaz	725	305
= light jonquil	727	293
= light camel	729	890
= orange	742	303
= light orange	743	302
= peach	745	300
= light peach	746	386
= light cobalt	775	128

	DMC	Anchor
= pink	776	24
= medium dark topaz	782	308
= light pink	818	23
= sapphire	826	162
= medium glacier blue	827	159
= medium blossom pink	899	52
= dark mint green	911	205
= medium mint green	913	204
= dark rust	922	1003
= denim blue	932	920
= copper	945	881
= medium light beige	950	4146

	DMC	Anchor
= medium jonquil	973	297
= medium mocha	975	355
= light rust	977	363
= light green	988	243
= medium light amethyst	3041	871
= avocado	3346	267
= medium light avocado	3347	266
= very light avocado	3348	264
= dark cherry	3705	35

Louis XVI Chairs Sampler

FROM MARY MILLER'S 1735 SAMPLER:

"No surplice white the priest could wear
Bandless the bishop must appear
The King without a shirt would be
Did not the needle help all three."

EMBROIDERY MEASUREMENTS

10-1/2 x 13-1/2 in. (27 x 34.5 cm)

MATERIALS

25-1/4 x 29-1/4 in. (65 x 75 cm) of Hardanger cloth with 23 double threads per inch (9 per cm); DMC or Anchor embroidery floss as indicated on the key to the chart plus dark brown #433 or #371, dark moss green #3011 or #846, medium sand #3045 or #888, wheat #869 or #944, and pewter #646 or #8581; a matching frame and mat, if desired.

DIRECTIONS

After marking the horizontal and vertical center of the fabric with basting thread, cross-stitch the motif following the chart, using two strands of floss over two double threads of fabric for each stitch. Where two colors of floss are listed, use one strand of each.

Embroider in outline stitch over completed cross-stitch using one strand of floss. For the bottom row of chairs, outline stitch in and around the wooden frame of the chair on the lower right in pewter #646 or #8581. For the chair at the lower left, use teal #807 or #168 to make the little star in the chair back with four large outline stitches and to top stitch the vertical lines in the seat. Top stitch the horizontal lines in the seat with two strands of brick #356 or #5975. Outline stitch in and around the sofa with medium camel #680 or #901.

Note: To top stitch, hand or machine sew a line of small, closely spaced running stitches on the right side of the fabric.

On the top row, outline stitch in and around the wooden frame of the upper right chair with medium sand #3045 or #888, and in and around the upholstery with aquamarine #3768 or #779. For the chair second from the right, outline stitch the feet with medium bark #301 or #349, in and around the wooden frame with fudge #838 or #380, and in and around the seat with moss green #3012 or #843. For the chair second from the left, outline stitch in and around the wooden frame with dark tawny #3021 or #905, and in and around the seat with two strands of very light turf #3047 or #852. For the armchair in the upper left, outline stitch in and around the wooden frame with dark brown #433 or #371, and in and around the upholstery with brick #356 or #5975.

For the border of the picture, use two strands of medium sand #3045 or #888 to make long outline stitches that angle from left to right, as the chart indicates, two cross-stitches in width and three cross-stitches in height.

KEY TO CHART

		DMC	Anchor
	= medium bark	301	349
	= brick	356	5975
	= turf	371	854
	= medium dark beige	407	914
	= tan	437	362
	= medium light teal	598	167
	= med. lt. teal/lt. denim	598/3752	167/343
●	= very dark fawn	632	936
∩	= sand	677	886
	= medium camel	680	901
•	= very light ecru	712	926
	= light sand	739	885
	= light peach	746	275
	= med. lt. terra cotta	758	337
△	= teal	807	168
∷	= light linen	822	390
	= dark saffron	832	907
◆	= fudge	838	380
/	= copper	945	881
	= moss green	3012	843
O	= light moss green	3013	842
▲	= dark tawny	3021	905
	= medium light sand	3046	887
7	= very light turf	3047	852
	= light denim	3752	343
	= aquamarine	3768	779

Tea Party Sampler

FROM A REVOLUTIONARY WAR–ERA SAMPLER:

"Excess of ceremony shews want of breeding. That civility is best which excludes all superfluous formality. Mary Varick. 1789. New York."

FRAMED MEASUREMENTS

7 x 12 in. (18 x 31 cm)

EMBROIDERY MEASUREMENTS

4 x 9 in. (10.5 x 23 cm)

MATERIALS

9-3/4 x 15-1/2 in. (25 x 40 cm) of Aida cloth with 14 thread groups per inch (5.5 per cm); embroidery floss as indicated on the key to the chart; if desired, a wooden frame 7 x 12 in. (18 x 31 cm).

DIRECTIONS

Mark the horizontal and vertical center of the Aida cloth with basting thread. Cross-stitch the sampler according to the chart using two strands of floss over one thread group of fabric for each stitch.

KEY TO CHART

		DMC	Anchor			DMC	Anchor
·	= white	white	1	⊠	= orange	742	303
●	= dark red	321	47	✚	= light orange	743	302
◣	= grape	340	118	■	= medium ocean blue	792	177
▲	= salmon	352	9	▢	= medium cobalt	809	130
△	= light salmon	353	6	✗	= dark mint green	911	205
×	= very light lime	369	1043	◆	= light blush	963	73
◉	= dark magenta	602	63	⊟	= light lime	966	240
❖	= medium magenta	603	62	△	= med. light turquoise	992	186
◈	= light rosebud	604	55	⊞	= very light jonquil	3078	292
✖	= medium spring green	703	238	▲	= dark cherry	3705	35
╫	= light jonquil	727	293	▫	= light blueberry	3747	120
✕	= dark tangerine	740	316				

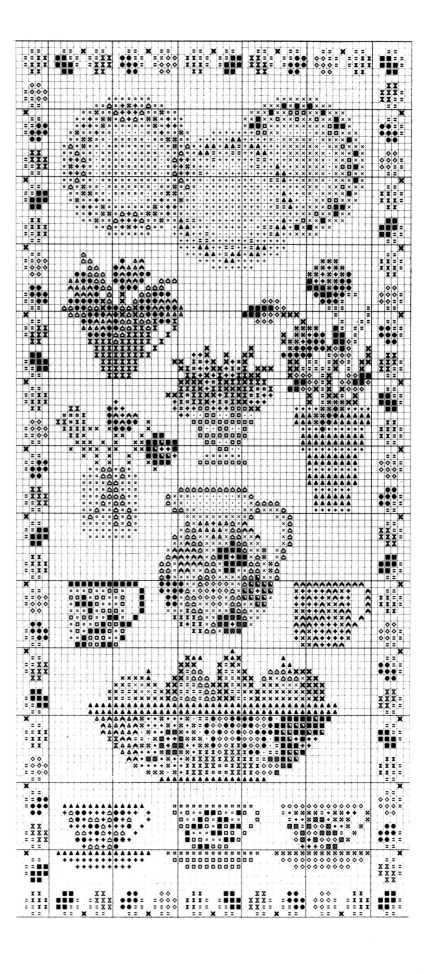

Lilies of the Valley Sampler

FROM MARTHA PERRY'S SAMPLER, ABOUT 1800:

"A blind woman's soliloquy.
Are not the sparrows daily fed by thee,
And will thou clothe the lillies and not me.
Begone distrust! I shall have clothes and bread,
While lillies flourish, and the birds are fed."

FINISHED MEASUREMENTS

10-1/2 x 14-1/2 in. (27 x 37.5 cm)

EMBROIDERY MEASUREMENTS

6 x 9 in. (15 x 23 cm)

MATERIALS

13 x 17 in. (33.5 x 44 cm) of white linen with 35 threads per inch (14 per cm); DMC or Anchor embroidery floss as indicated on the key to the chart plus slate #930 or #1035 and pink #776 or #24; frame (optional).

DIRECTIONS

Mark the center of the fabric with horizontal and vertical basting threads. Position point M at the bottom center. Using two strands of floss over two threads of fabric for each stitch, cross-stitch the motif according to the chart.

Embroider in outline stitch over completed cross-stitch using one strand of floss:

- in and around the bow with pink #776 or #24 and with slate #930 or #1035;
- along the leaves at the upper left with light yellow #445 or #288;
- and all remaining figures in dark mint green #911 or #205.

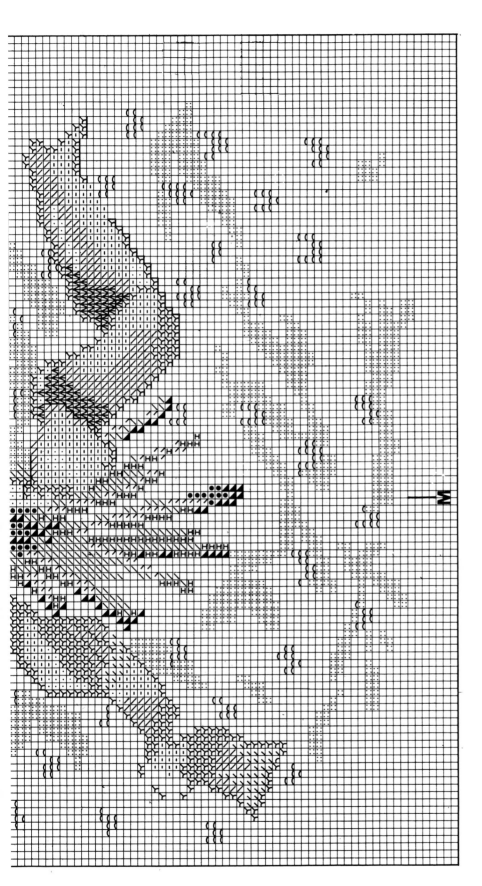

KEY TO CHART

	DMC	Anchor			DMC	Anchor
• = white	white	1		∷ = light peach	746	275
◡ = light wine	225	892		─ = light delft	828	975
◿ = very light lime	369	1043		▪ = dark mint green	911	205
◹ = light yellow	445	288		◡ = medium seafoam	928	274
● = avocado	469	267		◹ = very light beige	948	1011
◺ = light azure	519	1038		◹ = lime	955	241
◤ = dark forest green	561	212		◸ = peacock blue	996	433
◿ = medium dark olive	581	281		◿ = very light avocado	3348	264
H = medium spring green	703	238				

Brownstone House Sampler

"J. W. & A. PICKET announce to their friends and the public, that they have engaged an Instructress who is well qualified to superintend not only the manners and morals of female pupils, but also their instruction in the various descriptions of needle-work."

—BALTIMORE AMERICAN AND COMMERCIAL DAILY ADVERTISER,
SEPTEMBER 1821

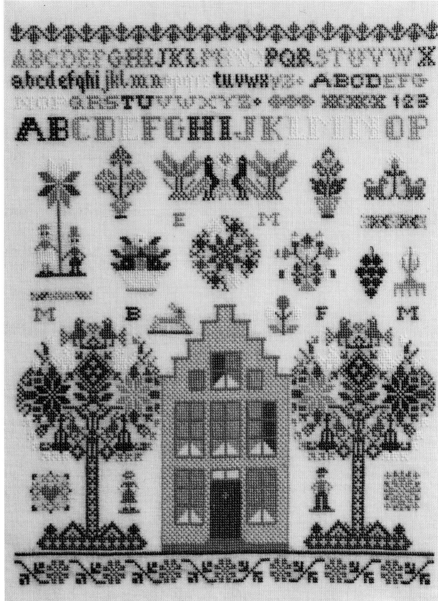

EMBROIDERY MEASUREMENTS

11 x 13-1/2 in. (28 x 35 cm)

MATERIALS

19-1/2 x 21-1/2 in. (50 x 55 cm) of ecru linen with 30 threads per inch (12 per cm); embroidery floss as indicated on the key to the chart; frame, if desired.

DIRECTIONS

Mark the center of the fabric with horizontal and vertical basting threads, then cross-stitch the motifs according to the chart, using two strands of floss over two fabric threads for each stitch.

Embroider the eyes of the figures at the bottom in French knots using two strands of dark mocha floss #433 or #357.

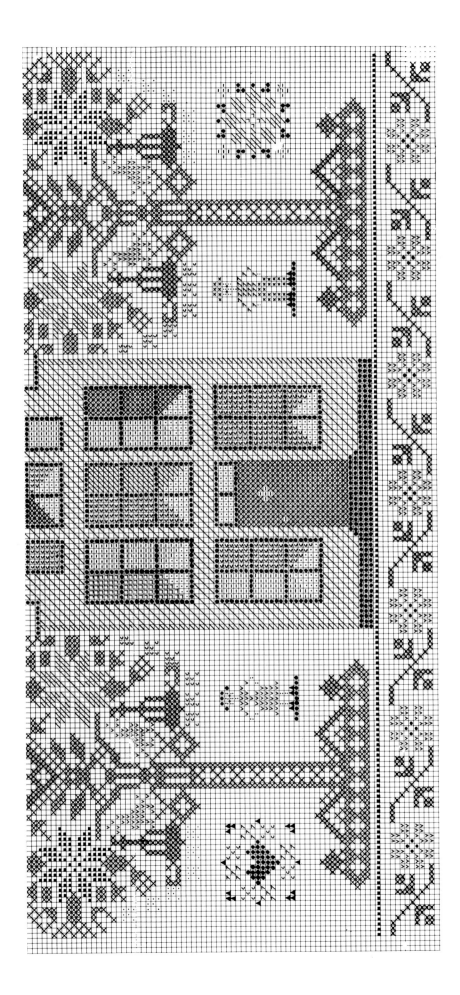

KEY TO CHART

	DMC	Anchor
⊠ = jade	320	215
Ⓒ = light gray	415	398
◢ = medium nutmeg	422	373
◤ = dark mocha	433	357
● = dark tan	435	365
∴ = light sand	739	885
· = medium peach	744	301

	DMC	Anchor
× = teal	807	168
— = medium glacier blue	827	159
■ = light slate	931	1034
∨ = dark antique blue	932	1033
⟋ = light mint green	954	203
⊠ = avocado	3346	267
☐ = very light avocado	3348	264

Alpine Flowers Sampler

FROM A SAMPLER BY TWELVE-YEAR-OLD
SARAH ANN BOYER OF COLUMBIA, PENNSYLVANIA:

"Sarah Ann Boyer . . . 1819
Ever charming, ever new
When will the landscape tire
the view"

FINISHED MEASUREMENTS

16-1/2 x 22-3/4 in. (42 x 58.5 cm)

EMBROIDERY MEASUREMENTS

10 x 16-1/2 in. (26 x 42 cm)

MATERIALS

25-1/4 x 31-1/4 in. (65 x 80 cm) of white linen with 28 threads per inch
(11 per cm); DMC or Anchor embroidery floss as indicated on the key
to the chart plus dark gray #414 or #235, coffee #433 or #358, dark olive
green #732 or #281, olive green #734 or #279, dark pine #890 or #879,
medium dark avocado #937 or #268, and light rust #977 or #1002; frame
(optional).

DIRECTIONS

Mark the horizontal and vertical center of the fabric with basting thread,
then cross-stitch according to the chart, using two strands of floss over
two threads of linen for each stitch.

Outline stitch over completed cross-stitch, using one strand of floss.
Outline stitches are indicated by DMC floss number on the chart itself.
For example, outline the leaves of the alpine aster with medium lime,
DMC #989 (Anchor #242); outline the centers of the edelweiss with coffee, DMC #433 (Anchor #358), and the edelweiss flower petals with
olive green, DMC #734 (Anchor #279). Outlines are not called for on all
flowers.

The number at the lower right of the square around each flower indicates
the DMC floss number to use for embroidering the square in outline
stitch, using one strand of floss. For example, outline the square around
the anemone in medium light green, DMC #987 (Anchor #244), and the
square around the silver thistle in dark pine, DMC #890 (Anchor #879).

KEY TO CHART

		DMC	Anchor
⊡	= white	white	1
◺	= jade	320	215
◆	= red	321	9046
⊘	= medium dark salmon	350	11
S	= brick	356	3975
∥	= medium dark beige	407	914
⬭	= brown	434	370
∧	= tan	437	362
⟋	= medium yellow	444	290
Ι	= light yellow	445	288
+	= chartreuse	471	255
−	= light chartreuse	472	253
■	= medium dark pine	501	878
E	= medium pine	502	877
∟	= light pine	503	875
◣	= sapphire	517	162
◥	= dark violet	550	101
⋈	= light violet	553	98
N	= lilac	554	96
●	= medium forest green	562	210
∨	= medium light teal	598	167
●	= light emerald	700	228
Z	= medium spring green	703	238
X	= light parrot green	704	256
⸪	= medium light jonquil	726	295
▱	= medium olive green	733	280
◹	= dark orange	741	304
⋱	= light orange	743	302
▬	= dark topaz	781	309
⟋	= very light pink	819	271
⟍	= medium glacier blue	827	159
⸬	= dark saffron	833	907
╱	= dark coffee	839	360
⊙	= fuchsia	893	28
⌐	= dark pink	894	26
⊠	= dark chartreuse	907	255
o	= medium turquoise	958	187
◿	= medium rust	976	1001
▲	= medium light green	987	244
⸰ and ◥	= light green	988	243
⹀	= medium lime	989	242

traveler's joy (old man's beard)

alpine aster

Dusty Miller

pillow plant

alpine primrose

spiderweb leek

KEY TO CHART

		DMC	Anchor
◵	= amethyst	3042	870
◩	= medium light orchid	3608	86
M	= med. light raspberry	3687	68
◷	= very light cherry	3708	31

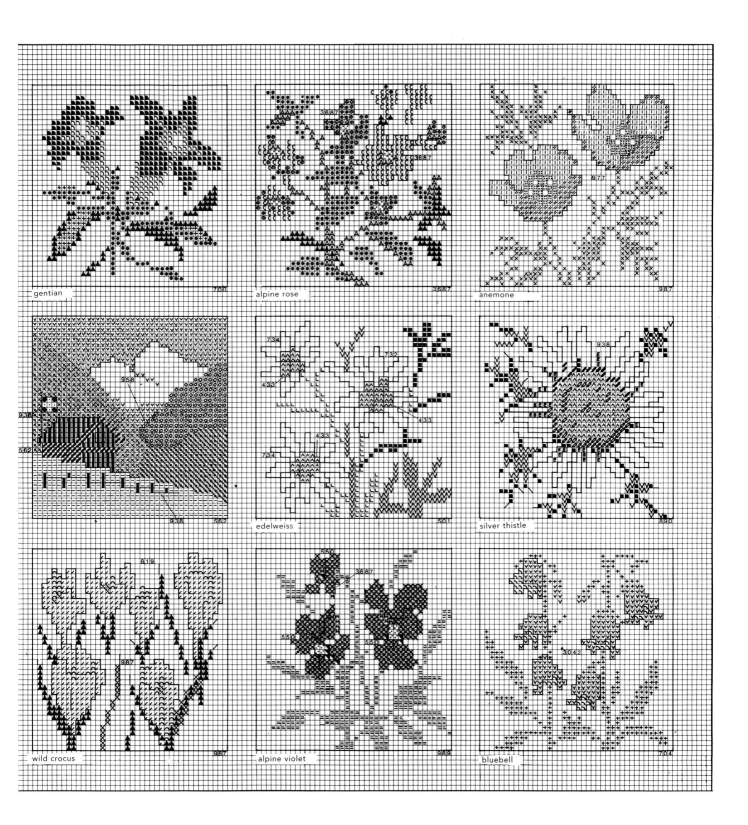

gentian   700

alpine rose   3687

anemone   987

edelweiss   501

silver thistle   890

wild crocus   987

alpine violet   989

bluebell   704

Iris Sampler

"Let the bright rosy morning
Call me forth to take the air
Cheerful spring with smiles returning
Ushers in the newborn year…
Wrought By Lucy D. Stickney
Charlestown November 18 1830 Aged 12"

KEY TO CHART

Symbol	Color	DMC	Anchor
	= light purple	208	110
	= dark lavender	209	109
	= lavender	211	342
	= grape	340	118
	= brown	434	370
	= light toast	436	1045
	= dark chartreuse	471	255
	= light chartreuse	472	253
	= medium pine	502	877
	= violet	552	99
	= lilac	554	96
	= dark forest green	561	212
	= medium forest green	562	210
	= med. lt. forest green	563	208
	= very dark fawn	632	936
	= dark linen	640	393
	= medium linen	642	392
	= camel	676	891
	= emerald	702	239
	= medium spring green	703	238
	= light jonquil	727	293
	= light camel	729	890
	= light loden green	772	259
	= topaz	783	307
	= dark blue gray	792	941
	= ocean blue	793	176
	= light ocean blue	794	175
	= dark chartreuse	907	255
	= terra cotta	921	338
	= dark aquamarine	924	851
	= med. lt. aquamarine	926	850
	= light green	988	243
	= medium lime	989	242
	= medium copper	3064	883
	= very light jonquil	3078	292
	= medium coral	3328	1024
	= avocado	3346	267
	= very light avocado	3348	264

FINISHED MEASUREMENTS

15-1/2 x 20 in. (39.5 x 51.5 cm)

EMBROIDERY MEASUREMENTS

10-1/2 x 14-3/4 in. (27 x 38 cm)

MATERIALS

23-1/2 x 27-1/4 in. (60 x 70 cm) of ecru linen with 25 threads per inch (10 per cm); embroidery floss as indicated on the key to the chart plus dark mint green #911 or #205 and dark rust #922 or #1003; frame, if desired.

DIRECTIONS

Mark the horizontal and vertical center of the fabric with basting thread, then cross-stitch the motif according to the chart. Work each cross-stitch using two strands of floss over two fabric threads.

Embroider in outline stitch over completed cross-stitch using two strands of floss:

- around the long leaf to the right of the iris bulb with dark mint green #911 or #205;
- around the yellow brown leaves above the large bulb with dark rust #922 or #1003;
- and around all remaining figures in the same color as the cross-stitching or one shade darker.

Embroider the words in stem stitch using two strands of grape floss #340 or #118.

Field Flowers Sampler

"In a dull company and in dull weather…it is ill manners to read; it is ill manners to leave them; no card playing there among genteel people…. The needle is then a valuable resource."

—THOMAS JEFFERSON TO HIS DAUGHTER MARTHA, 1787

FINISHED MEASUREMENTS

19-1/2 x 24-1/2 in. (50 x 63 cm)

EMBROIDERY MEASUREMENTS

15-1/2 x 21 in. (40 x 54 cm)

MATERIALS

29-1/4 x 33 in. (75 x 85 cm) of linen with 25 threads per inch (10 per cm); embroidery floss as indicated on the key to the chart; frame (optional).

DIRECTIONS

Mark the horizontal and vertical center of the fabric with basting thread, then embroider in cross-stitch following the chart, using two strands of floss over two threads of fabric for each stitch. Where two color numbers are given, use one strand of each color.

Embroider in outline stitch over completed cross-stitch. Use one strand of floss in and around the leaves. For all remaining outline stitches, use two strands of floss to stitch:

- in and around the stems of the blue cornflowers with medium camel #680 or #901;
- around the camel-colored petals of the poppies with medium salmon #351 or #10;
- the antennas of the butterflies and in and around the white flowers with gray #318 or #399;
- in the lower left flower with medium watermelon #335 or #38;
- around the yellow flowers with very light jonquil #3078 or #292;
- the beetle's antenna and legs with dark charcoal #413 or #401;
- and all other outline stitches in the same color as the cross-stitching or a shade darker.

KEY TO CHART

		DMC	Anchor				DMC	Anchor
·	= white	white	1	•	= very dark blue gray	792	941
	= light wine	225	892		= light ocean blue	794	175
	= dark bark	300	352		= light sapphire	813	161
	= yellow	307	289		= dark salmon	817	13
	= dark mauve	315	1019	■	= dark blue black	823	127
	= medium mauve	316	1017		= sapphire	826	162
	= gray	318	399		= dark saffron	833	907
	= dark grape	333	119		= medium saffron	834	874
	= med. watermelon pink	335	38		= dark nutmeg	869	375
	= grape	340	118		= dark nutmeg/med. rust	869/976	375/1001
	= light red	349	46		= parrot green	906	257
	= medium dark salmon	350	11		= dark chartreuse	907	255
	= medium salmon	351	10		= dark mint green	911	205
	= light salmon	353	6	▲	= slate	930	1035
	= brick	356	5975		= light blush	963	73
	= brick/moss green	356/3012	5975/843		= medium rust	976	1001
	= juniper	367	217		= light rust	977	1002
	= dark charcoal	413	401		= dark green	986	246
	= dark yellow	444	291	•	= medium light green	987	244
	= light yellow	445	288		= light green	988	243
	= avocado	469	267		= medium lime	989	242
	= light parrot green	470	256	⊙	= dark moss green	3011	846
	= medium light avocado	471	266		= moss green	3012	843
	= light chartreuse	472	253		= med. light amethyst	3041	871
▼	= medium dark pine	501	878	○	= medium copper	3064	883
	= medium pine	502	877		= very light jonquil	3078	292
	= light pine	503	875	C	= light watermelon pink	3326	36
	= dark forest green	561	212		= medium coral	3328	1024
	= camel	676	891		= medium melon	3340	329
	= sand	677	886		= light melon	3341	328
	= medium camel	680	901		= medium dark avocado	3345	268
	= medium spring green	704	238		= medium loden green	3346	262
	= very light ecru	712	926		= very light avocado	3348	264
	= medium apricot	721	324		= med. light raspberry	3687	68
	= light topaz	725	305		= light raspberry	3688	66
	= orange	742	303		= very light cherry	3708	31

Spring Birds Samplers

FROM A SAMPLER BY HANNAH WOLCOTT, WOLCOTT, MASSACHUSETTS, AGE FIFTEEN, ABOUT 1800:

"Hannah S Wolcott
On Music
Music the fiercest grief can charm
And fates severest rage disarm
Music can soften pain to ease
And make despair and madness please"

FINISHED MEASUREMENTS

About 8 in. (21 cm) each, in diameter

EMBROIDERY MEASUREMENTS

4-3/4 x 6-1/2 in. (12 x 17 cm) each

MATERIALS

For each sampler, 13-1/2 x 13-1/2 in. (35 x 35 cm) of linen with 35 threads per inch (14 per cm); embroidery floss as indicated on the key to the chart; a round frame, if desired.

DIRECTIONS

Mark the horizontal and vertical center of the fabric with basting thread, then embroider the motif in cross-stitch, using two strands of floss over two fabric threads for each stitch.

Using one strand of floss, embroider in outline stitch over finished cross-stitch in the same color as the cross-stitch or a shade darker.

KEY TO CHART ENGLISH ROBIN

		DMC	Anchor
●	= gray	318	399
□	= medium dark salmon	350	11
=	= medium salmon	351	10
⸫	= very light lime	369	1043
H	= brown	434	370
Z	= toast	435	1046
C	= light toast	436	1045
+	= tan	437	362
\	= light fog	453	231
▼	= avocado	469	267
◀	= light chartreuse	472	253
⊠	= light red orange	608	332
O	= dark tangerine	740	316
∷	= orange	742	303
−	= medium peach	744	301
		= light cocoa	754	1012
•	= silver	762	234
■	= dark coffee	839	360
Ø	= dark fawn	840	379
◢	= dark green	986	246
⊓	= light green	988	243
V	= medium lime	989	242
L	= very light avocado	3348	264

KEY TO CHART

GOLDFINCH

		DMC	Anchor				DMC	Anchor
•	= white	white	2	‖	= medium desert		612	832
■	= black	310	403	H	= medium camel		680	901
N	= gray	318	399	/	= silver		762	234
o	= medium salmon	351	10	/	= light sapphire		813	161
::	= light salmon	353	6	▼	= dark sapphire		824	164
⊓	= dark charcoal	413	401	□	= sapphire		826	162
⊟	= light toast	436	1045	·.	= light delft		828	975
●	= dark fog	451	233	—	= very light beige		948	1011
◢	= fog	452	232	v	= medium light sand		3046	887
Z	= light fog	453	231	∅	= medium light avocado	3347	266
⊠	= medium dark sand	610	889	L	= very light avocado		3348	264

Wildflowers Sampler

FROM A 1789 SAMPLER BY ELIZABETH RAYMOND:

"Lord give me wisdom to direct my ways
I beg not riches nor yet length of days
My life is a flower, the time it hath to last
Is mixed with frost and shook
with every blast."

FINISHED MEASUREMENTS

17-3/4 x 23-1/2 in. (45.5 x 60 cm)

EMBROIDERY MEASUREMENTS

15-1/2 x 21 in. (40 x 54 cm)

MATERIALS

25-1/4 x 31-1/4 in. (65 x 80 cm) of ecru linen with 26 or 27 threads per inch (10 or 11 per cm); embroidery floss as indicated on the key to the chart; frame (optional).

DIRECTIONS

Mark the center of the fabric with horizontal and vertical basting threads, then cross-stitch the motifs according to the chart. Use two strands of floss over two fabric threads for each stitch.

Embroider in outline stitch over completed cross-stitch, according to the Anchor floss number on the chart; use one or two strands as indicated with the floss number. For instance, the number 039 to the left of the fern at lower left directs you to outline stitch with one strand of dark watermelon (Anchor #39 or DMC #309); the number 371(2) to the right of the fern tells you to outline stitch with two strands of dark brown (Anchor #371 or DMC #433).

KEY TO CHART

		Anchor	DMC	Description
•	=	1	white	white
⊟	=	8	353	medium light salmon
⧄	=	33	3706	light cherry
◣	=	39	309	dark watermelon pink
◇	=	49	3689	light blossom pink
·	=	50	957	blossom pink
◢	=	52	899	medium blossom pink
◖	=	57	601	medium rosebud pink
◗	=	108	210	light lavender

		Anchor	DMC	Description
⊡	=	110	208	light purple
⊙	=	117	341	light grape
⌄	=	118	340	grape
◀	=	119	333	dark grape
∷	=	213	504	light jade
◺	=	240	966	light lime
∪	=	242	989	medium lime
⊠	=	243	988	light green
◣	=	244	987	medium light green

		Anchor	DMC	Description
⧄	=	254	907	chartreuse
⫽	=	255	471	light chartreuse
⧄	=	256	906	light parrot green
●	=	258	904	dark parrot green
◀	=	265	3348	very light avocado
⊟	=	268	937	medium dark avocado
=	=	280	733	medium olive green
⊠	=	295	726	medium light jonquil
+	=	300	745	peach

		Anchor	DMC	Description
⊓	=	301	744	medium peach
Z	=	302	743	light orange
○	=	368	945	dark spice
X	=	369	435	light brown
■	=	371	433	dark brown
⋰	=	372	738	light nutmeg
▼	=	375	869	dark nutmeg
◪	=	906	829	dark camel

Bellflower

Lily of the Valley

Speedwell

White Windflower

Solomon's Seal

Dandelion

Slender Cowslip

Wood Strawberry (Wild)

Ivy

Periwinkle

Wood Violet

Plantain

Rosehip

Daisy

Lesser Celandine

Foxglove

Male Fern

117

Garden Sampler Trio

"Keep clean your samplers, sleepe not as you sit
For sluggishness doth spoile the rarest wit."

—*A BOOK OF CURIOUS AND STRANGE INVENTIONS*
CALLED THE FIRST PART OF NEEDLEWORKES, 1596

FINISHED MEASUREMENTS

12-3/4 x 12-3/4 in. (33 x 33 cm) each

EMBROIDERY MEASUREMENTS

9 x 9 in. (23 x 23 cm) each

MATERIALS

For the 3 samplers: 1/2 yd. (.45 m) of linen 62-1/2 in. (160 cm) wide with 28 threads per inch (11 per cm); embroidery floss as indicated in the keys to the charts plus green #986 or #245.

DIRECTIONS

For one sampler, cut a square of linen 17-1/2 x 17-1/2 in. (45 x 45 cm). Mark the horizontal and vertical center of the fabric with basting thread. Cross-stitch the motif according to the chart using two strands of floss over two threads of fabric for each stitch.

Outline stitch over completed cross-stitch using two strands of floss unless otherwise indicated.

For the quotation sampler, outline stitch the letters and stem stitch the tendrils between the leaves with medium light avocado #3347 or #266 and outline stitch the remaining figures with one strand of green #986 or #245.

For the watering can sampler, outline stitch:
- around the leaves in the corners with light emerald #700 or #228;

- in and around the two flower pots with dark coffee #898 or #360;
- and all remaining figures with light charcoal #317 or #400.

For the flower pots sampler, outline stitch:
- in and around the medium mocha flower pot saucer and the large flower pot with one strand of black #310 or #403;
- in and around the two small flower pots with medium terra cotta #920 or #339;
- and all other elements with dark juniper #319 or #218.

Stem stitch the scrolls in the border with two strands of medium light forest green #563 or #208.

KEY TO CHART		WATERING CAN	
		DMC	Anchor
• = white		white	1
■ = light charcoal		317	400
= gray		318	399
O = delft		334	977
● = juniper		367	216
/ = medium jade		368	214
= light toast		436	347
T = chartreuse		471	265
= light chartreuse		472	253
= light jade		504	213
▲ = light emerald		700	228
/ = very light ecru		712	926
= medium light jonquil		726	295
◣ = dark coffee		898	360
= dark mint green		911	205
= medium terra cotta		920	339
= light copper		951	880
= light lime		966	240
✳ = medium mocha		975	355
= light silver		3024	397
✕ = med. light avocado		3347	266
= light brick		3778	337
= medium beige		3779	336
● = charcoal		3799	236

KEY TO CHART   QUOTATION

		DMC	Anchor
●	= juniper	367	216
◿	= medium jade	368	214
◠	= light chartreuse	472	253
•	= light jade	504	213
◼	= medium mint green	913	204
◺	= light green	988	243
⊠	= med. light avocado	3347	266
◖	= very light avocado	3348	264

KEY TO CHART   FLOWER POTS

		DMC	Anchor
◉	= black	310	403
◣	= light charcoal	317	400
∵	= gray	318	399
◼	= dark juniper	319	218
○	= delft	334	977
◺	= light toast	436	347
●	= avocado	469	267
⊤	= chartreuse	471	265
◡	= light chartreuse	472	253
◿	= med. lt. forest green	563	208
▲	= light emerald	700	228
◠	= medium light jonquil	726	295
•	= light orange	743	311
◣	= dark coffee	898	360
◺	= dark mint green	911	205
◢	= medium terra cotta	920	339
◺	= light mint green	954	225
◹	= medium mocha	975	355
◺	= light rust	977	313
⦂	= light silver	3024	397
⊠	= med. light avocado	3347	266
◖	= very light avocado	3348	264
◺	= light brick	3778	337
−	= medium beige	3779	336

Sunflowers Sampler

"Three Golden Rules
Worthy the observation of every one
Do everything in its proper time
keep everything to its proper use
Put everything in its proper place
Elizabeth Dore Aged 13
Portsmouth May 31 A.D. 1822"

FINISHED MEASUREMENTS

20-1/4 x 35 in. (52 x 90 cm)

MATERIALS

25-1/4 x 40 in. (65 x 103 cm) of white linen with 20 threads per inch (8 per cm); white sewing machine thread; Lingarn (or its equivalent) or DMC or Anchor embroidery floss as indicated on the key to the chart plus blossom pink #326 or #59, dark forest green #561 or #212, light red #666 or #46, medium spring green #703 or #238, dark coffee #839 or #360, medium light green #987 or #244, and medium melon #3340 or #329.

DIRECTIONS

Mark the center of the fabric with horizontal and vertical basting threads, then cross-stitch the motif according to the chart, using one strand of Lingarn or four strands of embroidery floss over two threads of linen for each stitch.

Embroider in outline stitch over completed cross-stitch using two strands of floss. Use dark tangerine (Lingarn #595, DMC #970, or Anchor #316) to outline the sunflower leaves, the stems of the reddish-orange flowers, and a few of the leaves at the bottom of the picture. For all other outlining, use a color that matches the cross-stitches or a shade darker.

FINISHING

For the openwork border, draw four fabric threads toward the corners, as follows:

- on the bottom and the left side, begin 23 fabric threads from the outermost cross-stitch;

- on the top, begin 33 fabric threads from the top-most cross-stitch;
- on the right side, begin 19 fabric threads from the outermost cross-stitch.

Leaving little end-pieces of thread sticking out at the corners, trim the fabric to 2-1/4 in. (6 cm) from the openwork border. Baste a 3/4 in. (2 cm) hem, with another 3/4 in. (3 cm) turned under, all the way around the piece. Finish the corners diagonally.

Fasten the hem with ladder hemstitches (see the Appendix) over four fabric threads. Weave the end-pieces back into the fabric.

Design Note: The sampler in the photo is embroidered with Lingarn, a very fine, tough, two-ply yarn or linen thread.

KEY TO CHART

		DMC	Anchor	Lingarn	
·	=	white	1	600	white
▨	=	309	42	572	dark rose
▤	=	335	38	573	med. watermelon
●	=	349	46	539	light red
◖	=	433	358	594	coffee
Z	=	471	255	625	chartreuse
◉	=	606	334	634	red orange
⊠	=	704	256	591	light parrot green
∣	=	726	295	504	med. light jonquil
◁	=	742	303	596	orange
◣	=	772	259	653	very lt. loden green
▷	=	783	307	660	topaz
■	=	814	45	637	dark carmine
−	=	818	23	532	light pink
∥	=	834	874	506	medium saffron
◿	=	970	316	595	dark tangerine
⬝∴	=	3078	292	666	very light jonquil
○	=	3326	36	576	light watermelon
▶	=	3345	268	627	med. dark avocado
◢	=	3347	266	589	med. light avocado
◺	=	3348	264	592	very light avocado

Romantic Age Sampler

FROM A NEW ENGLAND SAMPLER:

"O hills O vales whare I have strayd
O woods that rapt me in your shade
O scenes that I have wandered over
O scenes I shall behold no more
I take a Longe Last Lingering view
Adieu my native Land adieu
Elizabeth Brown's Work 1834"

EMBROIDERY MEASUREMENTS

18 x 21-3/4 in. (46.5 x 56 cm)

MATERIALS

25-1/4 x 29-1/4 in. (65 x 75 cm) of ecru linen with 25 threads per inch (10 threads per cm); embroidery floss or DMC crewel wool (or its equivalent) as indicated on the key to the chart; frame (optional).

DIRECTIONS

Mark the horizontal and vertical center of the fabric with basting thread and cross-stitch the motif according to the chart. Use two strands of embroidery floss or one strand of crewel wool over two fabric threads for each stitch. (The chart shows half of the flower border; turn the chart upside down and repeat this motif for the top of the sampler.)

Design Note: In the wreaths at the top of the sampler, the initials in the middle are the embroiderer's and those at the left and right are her parents'. These traditional designs are drawn from a German book of pattern samples and are also called "Berlin work." The sampler in the photograph is embroidered in wool on linen.

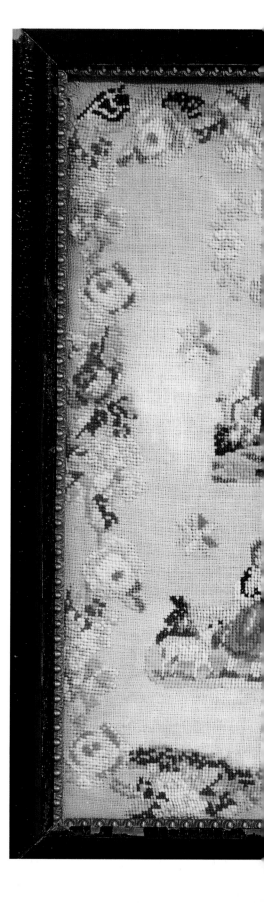

KEY TO CHART

		DMC Wool	DMC Floss	Anchor Floss
⌐	= very light beige	8101A	948	1011
●	= dark cherry	8102	498	1005
⊠	= very dark wine	8106	221	897
○	= wine	8107	224	893
◤	= medium copper	8108	3064	883
◥	= slate	8202	930	1035
⊙	= med. lt. aquamarine	8203	926	850
⊓	= dark seafoam	8204	927	848
⊔	= medium seafoam	8204A	928	274
◠	= light cobalt	8210	775	128
⊠	= medium bark	8301	301	349
+	= light camel	8303A	729	890
⟍	= medium harvest	8305	834	945
◢	= medium coffee	8306	801	359
⟍	= dark fawn	8307	840	379
7	= medium tawny	8308	3032	903
■	= medium gray green	8309	935	861
⋀	= nutmeg	8321	420	374
⊤	= light tan	8322	738	361
⋉	= medium camel	8324	680	901
∷	= sand	8327	677	886
◤	= dark gray green	8404	520	862
⊟	= med. lt. loden green	8405	3053	261
×	= moss green	8412	3012	843
╱	= dark moss green	8412A	3011	846
◣	= dark pine	8416	500	879
◡	= tan	8501	437	362
•	= ecru	8502A	ecru	387
∨	= medium nutmeg	8503	422	373
∥	= medium wheat	8504	422	943
╱	= copper	8504A	945	881
●	= dark blue black	navy	823	127

A

Roses Sampler

"While on my varied hues you gaze
And fancy beauty glowing there
Reflect! All beauty is but nought
Tis virtue that adorns the fair
M. Witmer
Philadela
Wrought 1828"

FINISHED MEASUREMENTS

17-3/4 x 21-3/4 in. (45.5 x 56 cm)

EMBROIDERY MEASUREMENTS

15-1/4 x 19-1/2 in. (39 x 50 cm)

MATERIALS

25-1/4 x 29-1/4 in. (65 x 75 cm) of white linen with 25 threads per inch (10 threads per cm); DMC or Anchor embroidery floss as indicated on the key to the chart plus medium coral #3328 or #1024 and medium light coral #760 or #1022; frame (optional).

DIRECTIONS

Mark the horizontal and vertical center of the fabric with basting thread, then work each cross-stitch with two strands of floss over two threads of fabric, according to the chart.

Use one strand of floss to embroider in outline stitch over completed cross-stitch in the same shade as the cross-stitching or a shade darker, unless a DMC floss number on the chart indicates otherwise. For instance, on Joanna Hill, outline stitch inside the large rose in medium rust (DMC #976 or Anchor #1001) and around the small rose in salmon (DMC #352 or Anchor #9).

Use one strand of floss to embroider the names of the roses in petit point (see the Appendix) using two strands of medium coral #3328 or #1024 over one fabric thread on the front of the work, and over two fabric threads on the back.

FINISHING

Use a drawn-thread technique for the openwork borders, whose locations are shown on the chart: for the outside border, draw two fabric threads out of the fabric, beginning and ending 1-1/2 in. (4 cm) from each corner and leaving 2 in. (5 cm) of uncut thread at each corner. Secure the remaining thread ends on the back of the fabric by weaving them back into the fabric for a few stitches, then snipping off the ends. For the inner borders around each rose, draw one fabric thread out of the fabric, then secure the thread ends in the same way.

Finish the drawn-thread borders with a ladder hemstitch (see the Appendix), using one strand of medium light coral #760 or #1022 over three fabric threads.

KEY TO CHART

		DMC	Anchor			DMC	Anchor
•	= white	white	1	o	= orange	742	303
	= light purple	208	110		= light orange	743	302
	= dark lavender	209	109		= medium peach	744	301
	= lavender	211	342		= peach	745	300
N	= med. watermelon pink	335	38		= light peach	746	275
	= light grape	341	117		= light glacier blue	747	158
•	= medium dark salmon	350	11		= light coral	761	1021
	= medium salmon	351	10		= silver	762	234
△	= salmon	352	9	−	= very lt. loden green	772	259
	= light salmon	353	6		= pink	776	24
	= juniper	367	217	▶	= dark salmon	817	13
∨	= medium jade	368	214		= light pink	818	23
	= very light lime	369	1043		= very light pink	819	271
Z	= brown	434	370		= medium glacier blue	827	159
	= dark chartreuse	471	255	■	= dark maroon	915	1029
●	= medium rosebud pink	601	57		= very light beige	948	1011
	= dark magenta	602	63		= medium light beige	950	4146
/|	= medium magenta	603	62		= dark blush	962	75
+	= light rosebud pink	604	55		= light blush	963	73
	= blossom pink	605	50	V	= medium rust	976	1001
▼	= very dark fawn	632	936	T	= light rust	977	1002
7	= camel	676	891	X	= medium lime	989	242
S	= medium camel	680	901	H	= light watermelon pink	3326	36
	= medium dark orchid	718	88		= med. dark loden green	3363	262
⊃	= light camel	729	890	=	= light loden green	3364	260
		= olive green	734	279	Z	= light cherry	3706	33

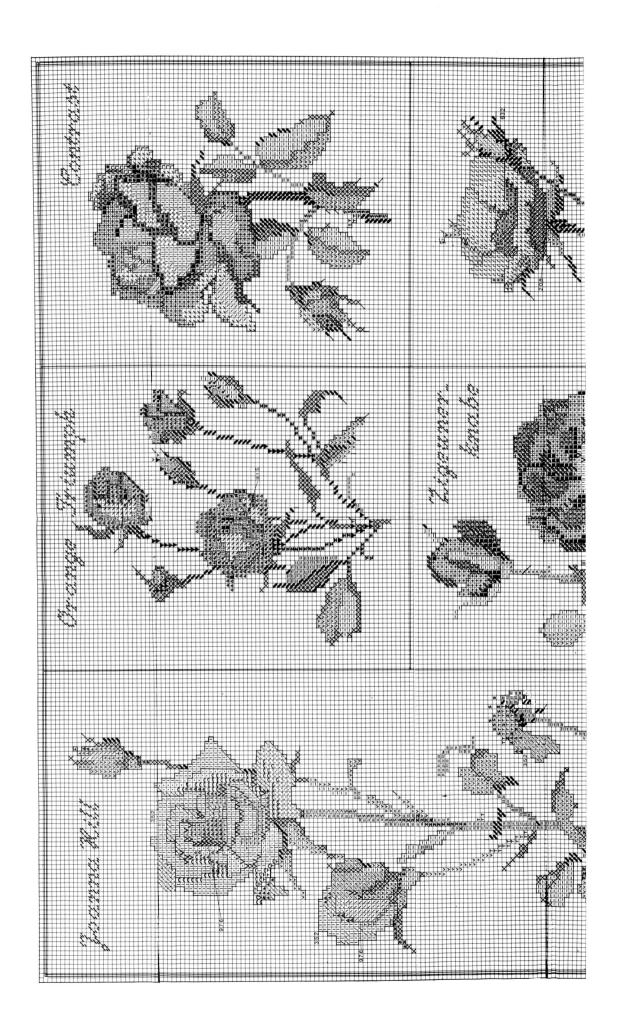

Cottage Garden Sampler

"Now when she had dined, then she might go to seke out her examplers...and to sitte her donne and take it forthe by little and little, and thus with her needle to passe the after noone with devising of things for her owne wearygne."

—BARNABE RICH, *OF PHYLOTUS AND EMILIA*, 1581

FINISHED MEASUREMENTS

Spring: 9-1/4 x 20-3/4 in. (24 x 53 cm)

Winter: 9-1/4 x 10 in. (24 x 26 cm)

Note: The spring scene is framed as a three-paneled, hinged picture. The two parts of the winter picture are framed on the backs of the two side panels. When the side panels are folded closed (in toward the center), they cover the central spring land-scape and form the winter picture. You thus have the option of stitching the spring picture only.

MATERIALS

1/2 yd. (.4 m) of white linen 63 in. (160 cm) wide with 28 threads per inch (11 per cm); DMC or Anchor embroidery floss as indicated on the key to the chart plus medium forest green #562 or #210 and light emerald #700 or #228; if desired, one frame 9-1/4 x 10 in. (24 x 26 cm), two frames 5 x 9-1/4 in. (13 x 24 cm), and four hinges.

DIRECTIONS

Cut the linen into four pieces 9-3/4 x 15-1/2 in. (25 x 40 cm) and one piece 15-1/2 x 15-1/2 in. (40 x 40 cm). Mark the horizontal and vertical center of each section of the sampler, and cross-stitch the scenes accord-ing to the charts. Use two strands of floss over two threads of linen for each stitch, except for the sky, which calls for one strand of floss over two threads of linen for each stitch.

Where the key to the chart lists two color numbers, use one strand of each color.

Embroider in outline stitch over completed cross-stitch using two strands of floss. **For the spring picture:**
- inside the windows with light peach #746 or #275;
- around the windows with light navy #797 or #132;
- around the pink flowers with very light cherry #3708 or #31;
- around the leaves and flowers with light emerald #700 or #228;
- in and around the flower pots with cinnamon #301 or #1049;
- around the watering can with black #310 or #403;
- and around the white, light peach, and medium light orchid flowers with medium forest green #562 or #210.

KEY TO CHART

		DMC	Anchor			DMC	Anchor
•	= white	white	1	◯	= blossom pink	605	334
⊞	= cinnamon	301	1049	**C**	= very light desert	644	830
■	= black	310	403	∨	= medium light pewter	647	1040
◢	= gray	318	399	◥	= light pewter	648	900
◠	= medium jade	368	214	●	= dark bottle green	701	227
◡	= very light lime	369	1043	◿	= medium spring green	703	238
◺	= light cinnamon	402	1047	◸	= light parrot green	704	256
▲	= dark gray	414	235	▢	= light apricot/copper	722/945	323/881
⬒	= light chartreuse	472	253	∴	= light tan/light sand	738/739	361/885
◠	= light azure	519	1038	∵	= light peach	746	275
⬓	= light forest green	564	206	∴∴	= silver	762	234

	DMC	Anchor		DMC	Anchor
= very light loden green	772	259	= light mint green	954	203
O = pink	776	24	= lime	955	241
= light navy	797	132	= light blush	963	73
= light wedgwood blue	799	136	Z = light rust	977	1002
∩ = light indigo	800	144	▲ = medium light green	987	244
= medium cobalt	809	130	= light green	988	243
= very light pink	819	271	= medium lime	989	242
= light delft	828	975	= medium light avocado	3347	266
= medium red orange	900	333	= very light avocado	3348	264
= medium mint green	913	204	= medium light orchid	3608	86
= dark rust	922	1003	= very light cherry	3708	31

For the winter picture, outline stitch:
- inside the windows with light peach #746 or #275;
- around the windows with light navy #797 or #132;
- in and around the flower pots with brick #356 or #5975;
- and around all remaining features with dark gray #414 or #235.

KEY TO CHART

		DMC	Anchor
•	= white	white	1
■	= black	310	403
◢	= gray	318	399
⊠	= brick	356	5975
▲	= dark gray	414	235
◖	= light fog	453	231
◣	= very dark fawn	632	936
∴	= light tan/light sand	738/739	361/885
∵	= light peach	746	275
⊤	= light cocoa	754	1012

		DMC	Anchor
◹	= medium light copper	758	882
∷	= silver	762	234
╱	= light cobalt	775	128
⊞	= medium light topaz	783	306
■	= light navy	797	132
◗	= light wedgwood blue	799	136
◺	= medium cobalt	809	130
▲	= medium light green	987	244
◭	= medium lime	989	242
=	= cobalt	3325	129

Stitches

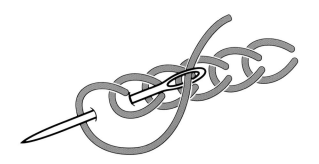

Chain Stitch

Stitched along a marked or imaginary line on your fabric, chain stitches are used for both filling and outlining. Bring the needle to the right side of your work along the line and hold the thread there with your thumb. Poke the needle back through the fabric very close to the same spot, then bring its point up a short distance along the line, looping the thread under the tip of the needle. Pull the thread through.

Repeat the stitch along the line, being sure to take the needle to the inside of the last loop each time you begin a new stitch. To finish a line of chain stitching, bring the needle through to the wrong side of the fabric on the outside of the loop.

Daisy Stitch

This single chain stitch is often used for flower petals. Use the same looping method as for chain stitch, but rather than working along a line, on the second stitch bring your needle to the right side of your work at the base of the next flower petal and continue by making a new stitch for each petal.

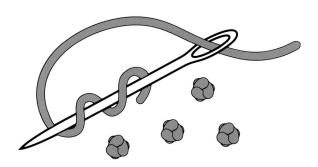

French Knot

The stitch of choice for eyes or flower centers, French knots add depth to your work. On the right side of your piece, wrap the thread twice around the point of the your needle, pull it tight, and insert the needle next to where it came out. Pull the excess thread through, at the same time holding the wrapped thread taut around the needle to form a clean knot. To make a larger knot, wrap the thread more times around the needle.

Stitches

Hemstitch and Ladder Hemstitch

A decorative stitch that is simpler than it looks, hemstitch or ladder hemstitch adds a special touch to an embroidered piece. Worked over an even number of threads (the project directions tell you how many), it gathers or circles thread groups for an openwork effect. For hemstitch, working from left to right on the right side of your work, bring your needle up from the wrong side two fabric threads down from the row you want to stitch. Slip it behind the first thread group from right to left, then insert it behind the same four threads, bringing it out two threads below the last thread. Draw the thread taut, bringing the fabric threads together. Continue along one side of the entire border.

To form the ladder rungs for ladder hemstitch, repeat the same process on the other side of the border, gathering together the same threads groups.

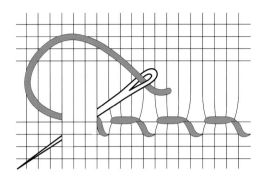

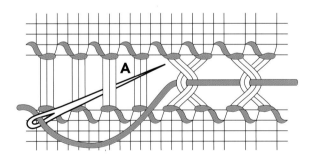

Interlaced Hemstitch

For this delicate border stitch, first work a ladder hemstitch. Then fasten a long thread at the right-hand side of your border. Pass your needle across the front of two groups of threads (ladder rungs) and then insert it from left to right under the second group, at A. Now insert the needle under the first group from right to left (B)—this twists the second group (rung) over the first group. Pull the thread through firmly so that it lies in the center of the twisted groups. Repeat with the next two thread groups (rungs).

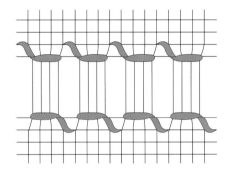

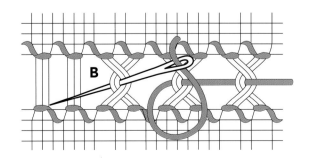

Stitches

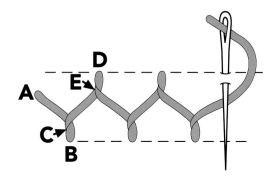

Open Cretan Stitch
(Flannel Stitch)

For this border stitch, bring the thread to the right side of your work at A, insert it at B and bring it back up at C. For the next stitch, insert the needle at D and bring it up at E. Space your stitches over an equal number of threads; all stitches lie at right angles to the imaginary guiding lines shown in the drawing.

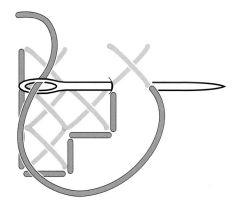

Outline Stitch

This useful and basic stitch, also called the back stitch, works for any outlining called for in the book. Bring your needle up on the right side of your work, just to the right of the figure you want to outline. Take a small stitch backward, then bring the needle up again in front of the first stitch, a stitch-length away. As you work around the figure, insert your needle each time at the end of the previous stitch.

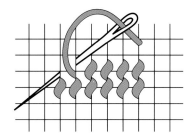

Petit Point Stitch

The most common canvas stitch, petit point's small diagonal stitches, which are formed like half a cross-stitch, should always lie in the same direction.

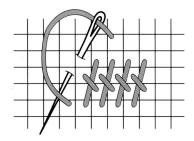

Rumanian Stitch

For this elongated cross-stitch, also called a knotted stitch, make a long slanted stitch, as shown in the drawing, then tie it down with a short, diagonal stitch across its center; bring your needle up for the second full stitch directly beside the beginning of the first, for a tight row of stitches.

Stitches

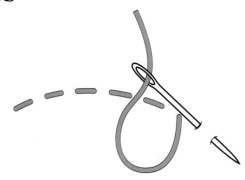

Running Stitch

To make this simple stitch, push the needle up and down through the fabric, crossing the same number of threads with each stitch.

Satin Stitch

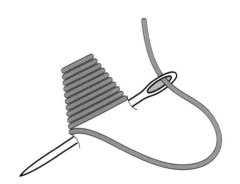

Often used for filling in flower centers, mouths, and other areas that need solid color, these flat, even stitches completely cover the fabric. On the right side of your work, bring the needle up at one edge of the area you want to cover and insert the needle directly across the area from that entry point. Make each stitch right beside the previous one, allowing no fabric to show through.

Star Stitch

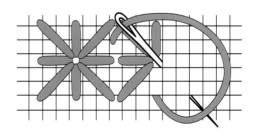

To make this decorative stitch, bring your needle down at the center of the star, up at the outer end of a ray, and then back down at the center; repeat for each ray.

Stem Stitch

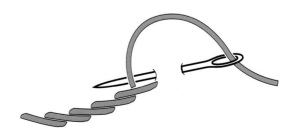

A popular stitch for outlining, stem stitches often appear in samplers for working the stems of flowers and leaves. Bring the needle up to the right side of your work along a marked or imaginary line on your fabric, insert it just to the right of the line, and bring it back up half a stitch-length back. As you work along the line, insert your needle each time at the end of the previous stitch for a continuous, braided look.

SPECIAL THANKS

to Shirley Turner of Cross Stitch Corner / Corner
Frame Shop, 856 Merrimon Avenue, Asheville,
North Carolina, for technical advice and for
the loan of some of the materials pictured
on pages 8–9 and on the endpapers.

SOME OF THE QUOTATIONS FROM
EARLY AMERICAN SAMPLERS
WERE DRAWN FROM:

Samplers: Five Centuries of a Gentle Craft, by Anne
Sebba (New York: Thames and Hudson, 1979);

The Sampler Book, by Irmgard Gierl
(Asheville, N.C.: Lark Books, 1984);

Historic Samplers, by Patricia Ryan and
Allen D. Bragdon (Boston: Little, Brown, 1992);
and

*Samplers & Samplermakers: An American
Schoolgirl Art*, 1700–1850, by Mary Jaene Edmonds
(New York: Rizzoli, 1991).

INDEX